Bruce Beasley

Skulpturen / Sculpture

Städtische Kunsthalle Mannheim
2.7. - 18.9. 1994

Yorkshire Sculpture Park
Spring 1995

Inhalt / Contents

Vorwort

Der 1939 in Los Angeles geborene und heute in Oakland lebende und arbeitende Bruce Beasley gehört seit vielen Jahren zu den bemerkenswertesten und innovativsten Bildhauern der amerikanischen Westküste. Schon als Student eregte er mit seinen dynamischen und raumgreifenden Skulpturen in der Tradition und Formensprache des abstrakten Expressionismus Aufsehen, was dazu führte, daß seine Werke schon sehr früh von vielen wichtigen amerikanischen Museen und Sammlungen, aber auch in Frankreich, angekauft wurden. In Deutschland zeigte Bruce Beasley seine Werke zum ersten Mal in der Ausstellung "California Sculpture Show", die 1985 in Kunsthalle Mannheim gezeigdert wurde.

Das Werk Bruce Beasleys ist seit der Mitte der sechziger Jahre gekennzeichnet durch sein ausgeprägtes Interesse für technische Experimente und neue Technologien, aber auch für den Aufbau von elementaren Strukturen, besonders von Kristallen. Seit den siebziger Jahren formt er seine Skulpturen aus stereometrischen Körpern zu raumgreifenden und dynamischen Strukturen, die er seit 1988 mit einem Computer entwirft. Dieser hat ihm die Möglichkeit eröffnet, seine Plastiken auf dem Bildschirm zu komponieren, die kompliziertesten Formentwicklungen und Durchdringungen zu untersuchen und auf ihre formale Stimmigkeit zu überprüfen. Schließlich bietet ihm der Computer die Möglichkeit, Zeichnungen als Vorlagen für den Bronzeguß herzustellen. In dem in diesem Katalog abgedruckten Interview mit M. Donahue beschreibt der Künstler die Vorteile, die ihm dieses neue technische Verfahren für seine Arbeit eröffnet.

Die Ausstellung der Kunsthalle kommentiert die neuen Bronzeplastiken Beasleys, in denen sich stereometrische Körper durchdringen und zu komplizierten, raumgreifenden Strukturen addieren.

Peter Selz, der die Arbeit Bruce Beasleys seit vielen Jahren begleitet, hat für den Katalog einen Text über die künstlerische Entwicklung und den Werdegang des Künstlers geschrieben. Ein Interview, das M. Donahue mit Bruce Beasley führt, gibt weitere Aufschlüsse über seine künstlerischen Intentionen, besonders über die Bedeutung, die die Verwendung neuer Technologien für ihn hat. Ihnen danke ich dafür. Dank gilt auch der Galerie Scheffel, die 1993 die erste Einzelausstellung des Künstlers in Deutschland durchgeführt hat, für ihre Unterstützung bei der Vorbereitung der Ausstellung. Ein besonderer Dank gilt dem Künstler, ohne dessen tatkräftige Hilfe die Ausstellung in der Kunsthalle nicht zu realisieren gewesen wäre. Die Vorbereitung der Ausstellung in der Kunsthalle lag in den Händen von Inge Herold und Hans-Jürgen Buderer, denen an dieser Stelle ebenfalls gedankt sei.

Manfred Fath

Preface

Bruce Beasley, who was born in Los Angeles in 1939 and lives and works in Oakland today, has been one of the most noteworthy and innovative sculptors on the American West Coast. Even as a student he generated excitement with his dynamic and space-enveloping sculptures in the tradition and style of Abstract Expressionism. This led to his works being purchased very early on by many important American and French museums and galleries. In Germany, Bruce Beasley first displayed his works in the "California Sculpture Show" exhibit in the "Kunsthalle Mannheim" in 1985.

Since the mid 1960s, Bruce Beasley's work has been characterized by his forthright interest in technical experiments and new technology and also by his involvement in the arrangement of elementary structures—especially crystals. Starting in the 1970s, he has created his sculptures starting from stereometric bodies and evolving them into space enveloping and dynamic structures that since 1988 he has been conceiving on a computer. This has given him the possibility of beginning his sculptures on a monitor, examining the most complicated spatial development and fusions and checking their formal precision. In addition, the computer also provides him with the opportunity to create drawings as patterns for pouring bronze. In the interview with M. Donohue printed in this catalog, the artist describes the advantages this new technological procedure opens up for his work.

The exhibit in the Kunsthalle expounds on Beasley's new bronze sculptures, in which stereometric bodies fuse and expand into complicated, space - enveloping structures.

Peter Selz, who has heralded Bruce Beasley's work for many years, wrote a commentary on the artistic development and curriculum vitae of the artist for the catalog. An interview conducted by M. Donohue with Bruce Beasley provides additional information about his artistic intentions with special attention paid to the meaning that new technology has for him. I thank them for that. Special thanks also go to the Galerie Scheffel, which held the first individual exhibit of the artist in Germany in 1993, and for their support during preparation of the exhibit. Special thanks also go to the artist, without whose hands on help the exhibit in the Kunsthalle would not have been possible. Preparation of the exhibit in the Kunsthalle was in the able hands of Inge Herold and Hans-Jürgen Buderer, whom we also thank here.

Manfred Fath

*Zwischen Expressivität und Konstruktion -
Konstanz und Wandel im Werk Bruce Beasleys*

I.

In Kalifornien bildeten sich in den fünfziger Jahren mit
Los Angeles und San Francisco als Zentrum der sog.
Bay Area zwei neue, eigenständige und von New York
unabhängige Kunstzentren, begründet vor allem durch
die Lehrtätigkeit bedeutender Maler des abstrakten
Expressionismus, die Ende der vierziger Jahre aus
New York nach Kalifornien gekommen waren. 1949
lehrten z. B. Clyfford Still, Mark Rothko und Ad
Reinhardt am San Francisco Art Institute und
vermittelten die Kenntnis des in New York
entstandenen abstrakten Expressionismus, der Action Painting, an die jungen Studenten, die sich unter
diesem Einfluß mehr mit Malerei als mit Skulptur
beschäftigten.[1] Das mag auch damit zusam-
menhängen, daß der Bildhauerei in Amerika erst seit
dem Beginn der sechziger Jahre größere
Aufmerksamkeit zuteil wurde. In Kalifornien wurde
die erste große Plastikausstellung 1967 im Los Angeles County Museum gezeigt.[2] Aus diesem Grunde
spielte die Bildhauerei zunächst eigentlich auch eine
eher untergeordnete Rolle innerhalb der kalifornischen
Kunstszene dieser Jahre. "If sculpture received any
attention at all, it was usually to lament its failure to
equal achievements of painting".[3] 1983 schrieb Jan
Butterfield: "Bildhauerei, die in Kalifornien geschaffen
wird, ist eine Ungereimtheit", und er bezieht sich
dabei vor allem auf die Tatsache, "daß ein großer Teil
kalifornischer Bildhauerei expressionistisch und
malerisch ist", was zweifellos auf den Einfluß der
New Yorker Action Painting und ihrer Vermittlung
durch Künstler wie Clyfford Still oder Mark Rothko
zurückzuführen ist.[4]

Erst zu Beginn der sechziger Jahre wandte sich das
Interesse der amerikanischen Kunstkritik verstärkt
der kalifornischen Kunstszene zu und Kalifornien
wurde mehr und mehr als das zweite bedeutende
Kunstzentrum der Vereinigten Staaten neben New
York anerkannt. Die kalifornischen Künstler
unterschieden sich von den New Yorkern vor allem
durch ihre Aufgeschlossenheit gegenüber unkon-
ventionellen neuen Materialien wie Kunststoff,

Glas oder Plexiglas, durch ihr Interesse für neue Technologien und technische Verfahren, ihr Bemühen, die Grenzen zwischen Malerei und Bildhauerei aufzuheben und ihr Anliegen, das Licht in seinen unterschiedlichsten Wirkungen in ihre Arbeiten einzubeziehen. Daraus entstanden Arbeiten, die, rein technisch gesehen, das Raffinierteste sind, was bis dahin hergestellt worden war, mit schärfster Präzision und äußerster Klarheit der Durchführung,[5] weshalb sie John Coplans als "fetish finish school" bezeichnet hat.[6] Allerdings benutzten die Künstler diese Materialien nicht aus einer unreflektierten Faszination oberflächlicher technischer Probleme - für die meisten Künstler hat die Technik keinen Eigenwert und das Material wird nicht einer beliebigen Geste wegen benutzt -, sondern ausschließlich zur Verfeinerung oder Verdeutlichung ihrer Konzeption.[7] Hier lassen sich interessante Parallelen zur Bedeutung Kaliforniens für die Entwicklung technischer Innovationen aufzeigen, die gleichzeitig hier entstehen. "Nirgendwo auf der Welt", schrieb Helmut Heißenbüttel, "wird heute eine Kunst gemacht, die sich so radikal gegen alle ideologische Verflechtungen absetzt, die zugleich den technischen Voraussetzungen unseres heutigen Lebens so sehr folgt, die so urban ist wie die der West-Coast".[8] Und: "Unbewußtes, Untergründiges, Psychoanalytisches spielt keine Rolle".[9] 1967 schrieb Lucy Lippard dazu: "Vielleicht der wichtigste Aspekt heutiger Bildhauerei ist ihre anscheinende Kapazität als Träger des Fortschritts - formal und evokativ oder sinnlich. ...Bildhauerei , die im realen Raum existiert, ist wirklichkeitsnäher als Malerei".[10] Das zwischen 1967 und 1971 vom Los Angeles County Museum of Art durchgeführte "Art and Technology" Programm verdeutlicht diese in Kalifornien besonders ausgeprägte Neigung, moderne Materialien und Technologien für künstlerische Projekte nutzbar zu machen.[11]

Helmut Heißenbüttel erkannte 1972 in der kalifornischen Kunst eine "Kunstvorstellung, die in sich einschließt das technisch Perfekte, das dinghaft Undurchdringliche und das intelligent Ironische. Das klingt abstrakt. Diese Abstraktion löst sich auf, wenn man sieht, daß Perfektion, Dinghaftigkeit und Ironie sich als Gebilde erweisen, die von höchstem sinnlichem Reiz sind. Daß alles immer wieder in äußersten sinnlichen Reiz verwandelt wird, daß es in diesem Reiz (nicht Effekt, wie zum Teil bei Robert Indiana oder Kenneth Noland) als etwas erscheint, das den Betrachter in eine neue Dimension versetzt, das ist vielleicht das Entscheidende, das man zu dieser Kunst sagen kann." [12]

II.

Seit der Mitte der fünfziger Jahre gewannen die Universitäten in Kalifornien mehr und mehr an Bedeutung als Ausbildungsstätten für angehende Künstler. Im Zuge dieser Entwicklung wurde Berkeley sehr bald zu einem wichtigen Zentrum, vor allem durch Lehrer wie die Bildhauer Peter Voulkos, Sidney Gordin, Richard O'Hanlon oder Harold Paris, die in ihrem Schaffen alle dem abstrakten Expressionismus verpflichtet und von einem experimentellen Geist geprägt waren.

In dieser Situation nahm der 1939 in Los Angeles geborene Bruce Beasley 1959 sein Studium an der Universität von Berkeley auf, nachdem er zuvor von 1957 bis 1959 bereits am Dartmouth College in New Hampshire studiert hatte. Er erkannte sehr schnell, daß sein Interesse sich ganz auf die Skulptur konzentrierte, weil er Objekte schaffen wollte, die seinen Intellekt, seine Vorstellungskraft und seine handwerklichen Fertigkeiten, über die er in hohem Maße verfügte, herausforderten. Die einzige Möglichkeit, diese drei ihm für seine künftige künstlerische Arbeit wichtigen Aspekte zu einer Einheit zu verbinden, sah er in der Skulptur.

In Berkeley, wo die Bildhauerei in diesen Jahren besonders gepflegt wurde, traf er auf eine Situation, die ganz geprägt war vom abstrakten Expressionismus. Aus diesen frühen Erfahrungen rührt wohl auch seine innere Bindung an diese Kunst, auf die er mehrfach verwiesen hat, auch wenn die formale Erscheinung seiner Werke dem zu widersprechen scheint. Seine Verbindung mit dem abstrakten Expressionismus sieht er selbst vor allem im prozeßhaften und spontanen Entstehen seiner Werke, aber auch in inhaltlichen Aspekten, die ihnen zugrunde liegen. Auf der anderen Seite steht das Werk Beasleys unverkennbar in der Tradition des Konstruktivismus, was seine seit den siebziger Jahren entstehenden Werke deutlich zeigen.

Es lassen sich eindeutige Beziehungen und Parallelen zu den Forderungen aufzeigen, die Naum Gabo und Antoine Pevsner in ihrem am 5. August 1920 in Moskau publizierten "Realistischen Manifest" für eine neue, zeitgemäße Skulptur aufstellten. Dort heißt es u. a.: "Die Lotleine in der Hand, mit Augen so genau wie ein Lineal, in einem Geiste, so gespannt wie ein Zirkel ... konstruieren wir unsere Werke wie das Universum das seine, wie der Ingenieur seine Brücken, wie der Mathematiker seine Formel der Planetenbahn".[13] In ihrer vierten Forderung an die neue Skulptur leugnen sie die Bedeutung der Masse für die Skulptur und weisen darauf hin, daß mit vier Flächen der gleiche Raumeindruck erzeugt werden könne wie mit vier Tonnen Masse.[14] Diese Neigung zu konstruktiven Gestaltungen findet auch in Beasleys ausgesprochenem Interesse für naturwissenschaftliche und technische Fragestellungen eine Erklärung, das ihn immer wieder zu technischen Innovationen bei der Realisierung seiner Werke führte und seit einigen Jahren auch zur Benutzung eines ausgeklügelten Computerprogramms, mit dem er seine neuen Arbeiten entwirft. Dieses Interesse belegt auch seine frühe Beschäftigung mit deutschen Texten des 19. Jahrhunderts zur Kristallographie. Die darin enthaltenen graphischen Darstellungen mineralogischer Strukturen als dreidimensionale und exakt vermessene Polygonalkörper, die die Gesetzmäßigkeit ihrer Formbildungen deutlich erkennen läßt, faszinierte ihn zutiefst und bestimmt die formale Gestaltung seiner Werke bis in die Gegenwart. In einem Interview mit Albert Elsen sagte er: "Die wichtigsten Quellen für mich sind das, was ich die elementaren Bausteine der Natur nenne. Man neigt dazu, sich unter natürlichen Formen Baumrinde, Wogen, Tier- oder Menschenkörper vorzustellen. Viel grundlegendere Formen der Natur sind jedoch kristalline Strukturen, molekulare Bausteine und Gerüste. Ich interessiere mich sehr für die Art und Weise, wie die Natur Dinge auf einfachste Formen zurückführt und wie sie zusammenfügt".[15]

III.

Schon sehr früh erregte Beasley mit seinen Arbeiten Aufsehen und erhielt bereits als Student Einladungen, wie z. B. zur berühmten Ausstellung "The Art of Assemblage" 1961 ins Museum of Modern Art in New York oder 1963 zur Pariser Biennale. Bald wurden seine Werke auch von wichtigen Museen erworben.

Die frühen Arbeiten Bruce Beasleys aus dem Anfang der sechziger Jahre, Eisen- und Aluminiumskulpturen aus Schrott und Industrieabfällen, die er auf Schrottplätzen sammelte, waren formal noch ganz geprägt von freien, expressiven und raumgreifenden Gesten, die allerdings in der Anordnung von Massen und Volumen bereits Ansätze strenger formaler Ordnungen zeigen. Das gilt ganz besonders auch für die in Aluminium gegossenen Skulpturen, die seit ca. 1963 entstanden sind und die er selbst in seiner eigenen Werkstatt hergestellt hat. In diesen Jahren war Beasley nach seiner eigenen Aussage beeinflußt von Malern wie Franz Kline und Bildhauern wie David Smith, deren Werke er wegen ihrer Meisterschaft und Präzision bewunderte, mit der sie Fläche und Raum beherrschten. In der Tat lassen sich Beziehungen zwischen David Smith's raumgreifenden und raumbeherrschenden Skulpturen und den frühen Arbeiten Bruce Beasleys erkennen.

Charakteristisch für die frühen Arbeiten Beasleys ist die Expressivität und Dynamik, mit der die Formen in den Raum ausgreifen, die Wirkung tänzerischer Leichtigkeit, die durch die Anordnung und Verteilung der Massen und Volumen innerhalb einer Skulptur erzeugt wird, ein Charakteristikum, das auch für die neuen Arbeiten des Künstlers gilt, deren Anliegen es ist, durch die ausgeklügelte formale Struktur den Eindruck aufzulösen, daß Masse, Volumen und Gewicht einander bedingen.

IV.

Gegen Ende der sechziger Jahre wandte sich Bruce Beasley einem neuen bildhauerischen Thema zu, der transparenten Skulptur, in der sich innere und äußere Form, Vorder- und Rückseite zu einer Einheit verbinden, einem Thema, mit dem sich in dieser Zeit viele Künstler in Kalifornien und Europa beschäftigten. Er entwickelte die Idee, Skulpturen zu schaffen, deren formale Struktur in ihren unterschiedlichen Ansichten für den Betrachter gleichzeitig zu erfassen war und für deren Wirkung das sich verändernde und reflektierende

Licht von entscheidender Bedeutung sein sollte. Für die Realisierung dieser Arbeiten dachte er zunächst an Glas als Material, ein Gedanke, den er wegen der Schwere des Materials und der Schwierigkeit seiner Bearbeitung schnell zugunsten von Acryl aufgab.

An einem Wettbewerb, den der Staat Kalifornien 1967 ausgeschrieben hatte, beteiligte er sich mit einem Modell aus Lucite, einem Acryl-Kunststoff der Firma DuPont. Er gewann den Wettbewerb und erhielt den Auftrag, sein Modell in den Maßen 274 x 457 cm auszuführen, was ihn zunächst vor schier unüberwindliche Schwierigkeiten stellte. Die Ingenieure der Firma DuPont hielten es für technisch nicht möglich, diese Skulptur in Lucite in den vorgegebenen Dimensionen zu realisieren. Beasley kaufte sich daraufhin einen Autoklaven und begann damit zu experimentieren. Nach achtzehn Monaten hatte er durch die richtige Verteilung von Hitze und Druck bei der Polymerisation von Lucite die technische Lösung zur Realisierung seiner transparenten Skulptur gefunden, die von den Technikern zunächst für unmöglich gehalten worden war. [16] 1970 wurde das Werk "Apolymon" schließlich in Sacramento der Öffentlichkeit übergeben, die es sehr enthusiastisch aufnahm. [17] "Das Werk", erklärte Beasley, "wurde von einer künstlerischen Vision von etwas Massivem und Klarem inspiriert, die beide die Durchdringung von Licht und Farbe dramatisieren. Apolymon tut genau das mit blendender Herrlichkeit. Tageslicht stürzt in die polierte Fläche des Werkes, scheint eine Zeit lang innerhalb seiner leuchtenden Masse zu schwimmen und bricht sich dann an den Oberflächen in Lichtflecken von gebrochener Brillanz und Farbe." [18] In einem in diesem Katalog abgedruckten Interview mit M. Donohue hat er darauf hingewiesen, daß sein Entschluß, mit transparenten Materialien zu arbeiten, ihn wieder mit dem Problem konfrontiert habe, daß Masse, Gewicht und Volumen sich gegenseitig bedingen. In seinen Arbeiten sucht er diese Bedingungen aufzulösen und Formen zu finden, die unsere Sehgewohnheiten und Erfahrungen in Frage stellen.

V.

In den siebziger Jahren schuf Beasley eine ganze Reihe transparenter Plastiken aus Lucite, die charakterisiert sind durch eine Verbindung organischer Formen, kristalliner Strukturen und strenger stereometrischer Körper in Gestalt von Polyedern, die er in den unterschiedlichsten Kombinationen miteinander verbindet. Diese Arbeiten wirken durch ihre Form, die sich immer wieder durch die Wirkung des Lichtes aufzulösen und zu verändern scheint und die es dem Betrachter oft unmöglich macht, die Grenzen der Skulpturen zu erkennen, Vorder- und Rückseite exakt zu definieren. Zu M. Donohue sagte er in diesem Zusammenhang: "Wenn Sie diese frühen transparenten Arbeiten betrachten, erkennen Sie, daß die Oberfläche nicht eindeutig festgelegt und transparent war. Weil das Werk beim Betrachten den umgebenden Raum und das Licht reflektiert, entstehen Fragen, wo es beginnt und wo es endet, nicht logisch, sondern emotional".

Aus der Arbeit an seinen transparenten Skulpturen entwickelte Bruce Beasley die Formen für seine nächste Werkphase. Zu Beginn der achtziger Jahre hatte er für sich die ästhetischen und technischen Probleme der transparenten Skulptur gelöst. Er wandte sich neuen Formen und Materialien zu. Es entstanden nun Stahlplastiken, die er aus einem Grundmodul aus sechseckigen blankpolierten Flächen aus rostfreiem Edelstahl aufbaute. Sie werden zu raumgreifenden Körpern und Strukturen zusammengefügt. Diese Sechseckform entwickelte er beim Bau von Gußformen für seine transparenten Skulpturen. Sie wurden nun für die folgenden Jahre zum alleinigen Ausgangselement all seiner Arbeiten. Damit baute er Hohlkörper, die er im Wechsel von geschlossenen und offenen Formen in einer additiven Anordnung zu dynamischen und raumgreifenden Strukturen zusammenfügte, die häufig eine gewisse formale Ähnlichkeit mit den großen Stabiles von Alexander Calder aufweisen. Charakteristisch für diese oft monumentalen Werke, die man als "kristalline Skulpturen" [19] bezeichnet hat, ist, daß die Anordnung der plastischen Formen häufig unserem Empfinden von Schwerkraft zu widersprechen scheint. Mit den Werken der siebziger Jahre verbindet sie eine gewisse Transparenz. Durch das Zusammenfügen der einzelnen Elemente zu Hohlkörpern entstehen geschlossene Körper und offene Formteile, die Durchblicke erlauben und so den umgebenden Raum in die Plastik integrieren. Die klare Oberfläche des rostfreien Stahls reflektiert Licht, spiegelt zugleich auch die Farbigkeit der Umgebung und führt so optisch zu einer Auflösung der strengen konstruktiven Strukturen dieser Arbeiten. Eines dieser Werke, "Artemon", 1984, war 1985 in der Ausstellung "California Sculpture Show" in der Mannheimer Kunsthalle zu sehen.[20]

VI.

Eine neue Werkphase im Schaffen Bruce Beasleys setzte im Jahr 1987 ein. In diesem Jahr wurde er zu einem internationalen Stahlplastik-Symposion in Krefeld eingeladen. Dafür schuf er ein Modell aus Karton - "Intersection" -, das in Krefeld exakt nach den Vorstellungen des Künstlers in Corten-Stahl ausgeführt wurde.[21] Mit diesem Werk beginnt eine neue Phase im Schaffen Beasleys. Seither entstehen Bronzeplastiken, die formal bestimmt sind von sich durchdringenden kubischen Elementen und geschlossenen stereometrischen Körpern, die die raumgreifenden Strukturen der vorausgehenden Stahlarbeiten weiterentwickeln. Dazu kommt, daß er seit 1988 ein hochentwickeltes Computerprogramm benutzt, mit dem er seine Plastiken entwirft. Es ermöglicht ihm, ausgehend von seinen bisherigen bildnerischen Erfahrungen zu völlig neuen Gestaltungen zu gelangen, und es eröffnet ihm die Möglichkeit, seine Werke nun durch das spielerische Aneinanderfügen oder Durchdringen von kubischen Formen von allen Seiten gleichzeitig zu entwickeln, um so zu neuen, unerwarteten und überraschenden Formverbindungen zu gelangen. Von großem Vorteil ist für ihn dabei, daß er mit dieser Methode immer die Möglichkeit hat, die Plastik von allen Seiten gleichzeitig auf dem Bildschirm zu sehen und ihre Form zu kontrollieren. Damit eröffnete er sich neue gestalterische Dimensionen, die dazu noch die Möglichkeit bieten, spontan auf unerwartete und innovative Formen zu reagieren. Den Arbeitsprozeß beschreibt er selbst als ein Zeichnen im dreidimensionalen Raum. Daraus entstehen seine neuen, komplexen Arbeiten mit ihren stürzenden oder steigenden, ineinander verschränkten Form-elementen, die sich in einer schwebenden Balance zu halten scheinen. Dabei arbeitet Beasley oft sehr lange an einem Projekt, bis er die Form gefunden hat, die seinen ästhetischen und formalen Vorstellungen entspricht. "Wenn ich am Computer arbeite", sagt er, "gibt es keine Frontansicht; ich arbeite immer gleichzeitig von allen Seiten". Und: "Neue Formen erscheinen durch Schnitte, die ich nicht kannte oder mir nicht vorstellen konnte. Der Kubus, der aus einem anderen herausdringt, ist nicht länger ein Kubus." [22]

Beasley hatte seine Skulpturen nie durch Zeichnungen vorbereitet, sondern immer an kleinen Modellen entwickelt. Die Arbeit am Computer eröffnet ihm nun die Möglichkeit, seine plastischen Ideen viel schneller als früher zu realisieren. Die mühsame Herstellung eines Modells als Medium der Überprüfung einer plastischen Idee oder als Vorlage für die Realisierung in größerem Maßstab entfällt, was er als den größten Vorteil dieser Methode bezeichnet. Er war, wie er im Interview mit M. Donohue sagt, unzufrieden mit dem langsamen Entstehungsprozeß seiner Werke und suchte eine Möglichkeit, seine Modelle schneller zu realisieren. Der Computer erlaubt ihm, eine Vielzahl von Varianten auf ihre Realisierbarkeit hin auf dem Bildschirm zu untersuchen. Er vergleicht die Arbeit am Computer mit dem Zeichnen in einem dreidimensionalen Raum, mit dem er spontaner als früher arbeiten und schnellere Lösungen seiner bildnerischen Probleme finden kann.

Wenn eine Form seinen Vorstellungen entspricht, werden die einzelnen Elemente mit einem Plotter exakt auf "foam core" - einen polyesterbeschichteten Karton - übertragen, und daraus entsteht dann ein Modell, das er meist über einen längeren Zeitraum in seinem Atelier aufbewahrt und immer wieder auf seine Stimmigkeit kontrolliert, bis er es für den Bronzeguß freigibt. Dieses Verfahren gilt vor allem für die kleineren Arbeiten, die Beasley in Bronze gießen läßt. Für die großen Arbeiten wählt Beasley ein anderes Verfahren. Bei diesen werden die einzelnen Formteile ebenfalls mit dem Plotter auf "foam core" übertragen, die als Gußformen für Bronzeplatten dienen, aus denen er die Skulpturen dann in seinem Atelier in einem technisch sehr aufwendigen Verfahren zusammenfügt. Sowohl für die gegossenen kleineren Arbeiten als auch für die aus Bronzeplatten zusammengefügten großen gibt es Beispiele in unserer Ausstellung.

Große Sorgfalt verwendet Beasley nicht nur auf die technisch perfekte Ausführung seiner Skulpturen, sondern auch auf die Gestaltung der Oberfläche. Er versieht sie häufig mit sorgfältig ausgeführten, sehr differenzierten Texturen oder Strukturen, um unterschiedliche Oberflächenwirkungen zu erzielen, und er patiniert seine Arbeiten selbst mit sehr verschiedenen Farbtönen, hell oder dunkel, deren Farbskala von rot über ocker bis zu blau und grün reichen kann. Die Patina ist für Beasley ein integraler Bestandteil seiner Werke. Durch diese Farbigkeit, die von ihm gezielt eingesetzt wird, um bestimmte emotionale Wirkungen zu erreichen, gewinnen seine Werke ihren eigentümlichen Reiz. Damit steht Bruce Beasley in einer für die kalifornischen Kunst charakteristischen Tradition, die der Oberflächengestaltung große Aufmerksamkeit widmet.

Die formalen Anregungen für seine Arbeiten haben unterschiedliche Quellen. Meist sind es Naturformen, wie z. B. die großen, bizarren Felsformationen des Monument Valley in Arizona, oder aber Kristalle, molekulare Strukturen oder Knochen, die den schöpferischen Prozeß auslösen. Ausgehend von einfachsten stereometrischen Körpern wie Kuben, Pfeilern, Säulen, Kugeln oder Scheiben schafft er durch Kombinationen und Durchdringungen seine neuen Plastiken, die entweder von blockhafter und statischer Geschlossenheit oder von raumgreifender und die Schwerkraft scheinbar negierender und labiler Dynamik sind, wobei deren formale Anordnung mit ihrer Aneinanderreihung sich durchdringender Körper häufig einen kaleidoskopartigen Ablauf assoziiert.

Bruce Beasleys Arbeiten sind raumgreifend und raumdefinierend. In seiner Auseinandersetzung mit räumlichen Problemen lassen sich Beziehungen zu Eduardo Chillida aufzeigen, dessen Schaffen er sich sehr verpflichtet fühlt und mit dem er freundschaftlich verbunden ist. Er möchte mit seinen Plastiken Raum als etwas Dynamisches erfahrbar machen, das durch Massen und Volumen definiert wird, die den Eindruck von Ruhe oder Bewegung erzeugen. Im Interview mit M. Donohue erläutert er ausführlich, daß ihm dieser emotionale Aspekt seiner Arbeit besonders wichtig ist. Je mehr er sich auf den emotionalen Aspekt der Formen konzentriert, umso besser wird nach seiner Meinung die Plastik.

VII.

Überblickt man das bildhauerische Werk Bruce Beasleys, kann man feststellen, daß er sich immer in einem Rhythmus von ca. zehn Jahren neuen Materialien und neuen formalen Problemen zuwendet. In den sechziger Jahren arbeitete er mit geschmiedetem Eisen und Aluminiumgüssen nach Industrieabfällen, in den siebziger Jahren mit transparenten Materialien, in den achtziger Jahren baute er raumgreifende Stahlplastiken auf der Basis von Sechseckformen, die dann durch seine mit dem Computer entwickelten kubischen Bronzeplastiken abgelöst wurden, die hier in dieser Ausstellung zu sehen sind. Diese Veränderungen sind immer Folgen einer intellektuellen Entwicklung und nicht nur das Ergebnis formaler Neuansätze, die auch neue Materialien bedingen. Konstant bleibt immer, daß seine Arbeiten in einem prozeßhaften Vorgehen entstehen, das an die künstlerischen Vorgehensweisen der Künstler des abstrakten Expressionismus erinnert, auch wenn er sie in den letzten Jahren mit dem Computer konzipiert, während er formal in der Tradition des Konstruktivismus und verwandter künstlerischer Tendenzen steht.

Der Ursprung seiner bildnerischen Gestaltungen liegt immer in der Natur. Seien es kristalline Gebilde, Fossilien oder Knochen, die er studiert, um zu verstehen, wie sich die Einzelteile zu einem Ganzen fügen. Seine Skulpturen fügt er ebenfalls aus Einzelelementen so zusammen, daß sie als Ganzes stimmig erscheinen. Im Interview mit M. Donohue sagte er: "Es gibt eine enge Parallele zwischen dem Erfolg in der Natur und dem Erfolg in der Kunst. In beiden ist der Erfolg erreicht, wenn nichts mehr hinzugefügt werden kann ..., wenn alles den Eindruck vermittelt, da zu sein, wo es hingehört."[23]

Manfred Fath

1. Vgl. z. B. Jones, C. A., Bay Area Figurative Art, 1950 - 1965, Berkeley und Los Angeles 1990 - Joachimides, C.M. und Rosenthal,N., Amerikanische Kunst im 20. Jahrhundert, Malerei und Plastik, München 1993, S. 97 ff. - Hopkins, H. T., California Painters: New York, San Francisco 1989.

2. Kat. American Sculpture of the Sixties, Los Angeles County Museum, Los Angeles 1967.

3. Anderson, W. , American Sculpture in Process: 1930/ 1970, New York 1975, S. 175.

4. Butterfield, J., Bildhauerei ist wirklichkeitsnäher als Malerei, in: California Sculpture Show, Los Angeles, Bordeaux, Mannheim, West Bretton, Oslo, 1984/85, S. 25.

5. Weiner, H., Die Schule von Los Angeles, in: Kat.: 1972 - USA West Coast, Hamburg, Hannover, Köln, Stuttgart 1972, S. 113.

6. Hopkins, S. 10 - Vgl. auch Coplans, J., The New Sculpture and Technology, in: Kat. American Sculpture of the Sixties, S. 21 ff.

7. Weiner, S. 114.

8. Heißenbüttel, H., West-Coast und neue Ästhetik, in: 1972 - USA West Coast, S. 11.

9. Ders., S. 10

10. Lippard, L., Kat. California Sculpture Show, S. 25.

11. Vgl. A Report on the Art and Technology Program of the Los Angeles County Museum 1967 - 1971, Los Angeles 1971.

12. Heißenbüttel. S. 11.

13. Gabo, N. und Pevsner, A., Das Realistische Manifest, in: Naum Gabo, Sechzig Jahre Konstruktivismus, hg. Nash, St. A. und Merkert, J., München 1986.

14. Ebenda

15. Elsen, A. A., Bruce Beasley's Personal "Cubism": 1987 - 1990, in: Kat. Bruce Beasley, An Exhibition of Bronze Sculpture, 1990/1991, S. 5.

16. Kat. California Sculpture Show, S. 66.

17. Ebenda.

18. Ebenda.

19. Kat. California Sculpture Show, S. 37.

20. Kat. California Sculpture Show, Abb. S.

21. Kat. Krefeld

22. Vgl. Fath. M., "Der einzige Grund, warum ich Künstler bin, ist die Freude, zu entdecken, daß ich neue Formen schaffen kann", In: Kat. Bruce Beasley, Bad Homburg 1993, O. S.

23. Sandler, I., Gesture and Non-Gesture in Recent-Sculpture, in: American Sculpture of the Sixties, S. 40 ff.

Between Expression and Construction —
Consistency and Change in the Work of
Bruce Beasley

I.

In the 1950s, two distinct new art centers independent of New York came into being. These centers were in Los Angeles and primarily San Francisco. A Loose style called the Bay Area Movement evolved from the teachings of significant Abstract Expressionist painters who had come to California from New York at the end of the 1940s .[1] Clyfford Still, Mark Rothko and Ad Reinhardt taught at the San Francisco Art Institute in 1949 and passed on ideas about expressionism and action painting prominent in New York at this time. However as these ideas took seed on the West Coast, young artists began to apply them more to sculpture than painting. [2]

Sculpture only began to receive the attention that it deserved in the United States starting in the 1960s, and the first large sculpture exhibit in California did not take place until 1967 at the Los Angeles County Museum of Art.[3] For the most part, sculpture played a secondary role in the California art scene of this period. "If sculpture received any attention at all, it was usually to lament its failure to equal the achievements of painting"[3] . In 1983, Jan Butterfield wrote, "Sculptures created in California are an anomaly", continuing, "a great deal of California sculpture is expressionistic and painterly" referring again to the overriding influence of "action painting" from New York and its propagation by artists such as Clyfford Still and Mark Rothko and its impact on both painting and sculpture on the West Coast.[4]

Only at the start of the 1960s with this growing breed of second generation West Coast expressionists did critics turn increasingly to the art scene in California. California was recognized more and more as the second most important center of the arts in the United States after New York. California artists differed from those in New York primarily by their discovery of unconventional new materials such as plastic, glass or plexiglass as well as their interest in new technology and technical procedures. The West Coast artists were also characterized by a desire to eliminate the borders between painting and sculpture, and incorporate light in its diverse effects into their work. The works that originated from these concerns showed keen precision and a clarity of execution, and were in the end the most innovative sculptural statements being created to date.[5] John Coplans defined it as the "fetish finish (sic) school."[6] However, the artists did not utilize these materials as the result of an unthoughtful fascination with superficial technical problems. For most artists, that worked and continue to work in this way, the technology had and has no independent value and the material is utilized to refine or clarify their conception. [7] In this concern, interesting parallels may be drawn with regard to California and the development of technical innovation. Helmut Heißenbüttel wrote, "Nowhere in the world is art being produced that differs so radically from all ideological roots and that follows the technical dictates of our contemporary life so closely and is yet so urban as West Coast Art."[8] Heißenbüttel continues, "The unconscious, the underground and the psychoanalytical no longer play a part "[9] In 1967, Lucy Lippard writing on this subject wrote, "Perhaps the most important aspect of sculpture today is its apparent potential as a vehicle of advance - both formal and evocative, or sensuous...Sculpture existing in real space and physically autonomous is realer than painting"[10] The "Art and Technology" program conducted by the Los Angeles County Museum of Art between 1967 and 1971 epitomizes this especially marked tendency in California to utilize modern materials and technology for artistic projects.[11]

In 1972, Helmut Heißenbüttel recognized a "vision of art that incorporates in itself technological perfection, the impregnable objective and the intelligent in California art. That sounds abstract. This abstraction disappears when one sees that perfection, tangibility and irony gain credibility as an object with the highest sensual appeal. Everything is again transformed into an extremely sensual attraction that transports the observer into a new dimension as opposed to an effect as is partially the case with Robert Indiana or Kenneth Noland. Perhaps that is the most definitive thing one can say about this art."[12]

II.

Since the middle of the 1950s, universities in California gained more and more importance as training centers for aspiring artists. Following this development, Berkeley quickly became an important center, primarily due to such teachers as the sculptors Peter Voulkos, Sidney Gordin, Richard O'Hanlon and Harold Paris, whose work was dedicated to Abstract Expressionism and which was distinctly guided by an experimental spirit.

Under these circumstances, Bruce Beasley—born in Los Angeles in 1939—began his course of studies at the University of Berkeley, after having previously studied for two years (1957-59) at Dartmouth College in New Hampshire. Quite early his interest was drawn to sculpture because he wanted to create objects that challenged his intellect, his creative drive and his skilled manual abilities—to the greatest extent of his abilities. The only venue he saw of combining these three elements was through a career as a sculptor.

In Berkeley, where sculpture was especially respected during these years, he found himself in a situation dominated by Abstract Expressionism. His bond with this art form most likely stems from early formative experiences with expressionism which he repeatedly refers to, although the formal surface appearance of his works might appear to contradict that school, he himself acknowledges his attachment with Abstract Expressionism primarily in the procedural and spontaneous origin of his works, but also with respect to content.

On the other hand, Beasley's work is unmistakably anchored in the tradition of Constructivism, and his works created since the 1970s strongly demonstrate this. Clear relationships and parallels to the fundamentals mandated by Naum Gabo and Antoine Pevsner in their "Realist Manifesto" for a new, contemporary sculpture published in Moscow on August 5, 1920 can be drawn. It is stated there, "The plumb bob in hand, eyes as straight as a ruler, in a spirit taut as a circle... we craft our works as the universe does, like the engineer constructs bridges and like a mathematician calculates his formula for a planetary orbit."[13] In the fourth manifesto prerequisite for sculpture, they deny the meaning of mass for sculpture and emphasize that the same spatial impression can be created with four surfaces as with four tons of mass.[14] This tendency for constructivist compositions is also explained in Beasley's outspoken interest in issues of natural science and technology that inspired him again and again to technological innovation in the creation of his works and—has for some years—pushed him toward the use of sophisticated computer programs to compose his new works. This interest is also reflected in his involvement with 19th century German language texts on crystallography. The graphic representations of mineralogical structures as three dimensional and exactly measured polygonal bodies that clearly depicted the regularity of their physical construction contained therein fascinated him infinitely and influences the composition and sensibility of his works to the present day. In an interview with Albert A. Elsen, he said, "The major source materials for me are what I call the elemental building blocks of nature. People tend to think of natural forms as being tree bark, waves, the bodies of animals, or people, but much more basic forms of nature are crystalline structures, molecular building blocks, and bones. I am very interested in the way nature refines things down to very simple forms, and how she joins them together".[15]

III.

Quite early on, Beasley's work generated interest and, even as a student, his work was selected to be shown in , for example, the famous 1961 exhibit "The Art of Assemblage" in the Museum of Modern Art in New York and to the "Biennale" in Paris in 1963. Shortly after, his works were also being acquired by important museums.

Beasley's early works from the 1960s consist of iron and aluminum sculptures made of industrial scrap he collected at junkyards and these remained formally governed by free, expressive and expanse - enveloping movements that continued to demonstrate a concern with strictly formal placement in their arrangement of mass and volume. These observations apply especially to the sculptures cast of aluminum that originated since 1963 that he cast in his own studio. According to Beasley, he was influenced during those years by painters such as Franz Kline and sculptors

such as David Smith, whose works he admired for their master craftsmanship and the precision with which they dominated surface and space. In fact, there are recognizable relationships between David Smith's space - enveloping and space - dominating sculptures and Beasley's early works.

The expressiveness and dynamic manner in with which forms extend into space is characteristic of Beasley's early works, as is a kind of romping lightness generated by the arrangement and distribution of mass and volume within a sculpture. This characteristic also applies to the artist's new works. With an ingenious formal structure, the impression that mass, volume and gravity influence each other is obliterated.

IV.

Toward the end of the 1960s, Bruce Beasley turned to a new sculptural theme—that of transparent sculpture in which internal and external form and the front and back form a unit. At this time, many artists in California and Europe were working with this theme. He pioneered the idea of creating sculptures with formal structures that could be simultaneously observed in multiple views and for which changing and reflecting light was of decisive importance for their effect. He originally considered glass as a material for carrying out this work but quickly gave up that thought in favor of acrylic because of the weight of glass and the difficulty of processing it. He entered a Lucite model- an acrylic plastic manufactured by Du Pont - in a competition sponsored by the State of California in 1967 and won the competition. He received a commission to produce his model in a nine foot by fifteen foot size. Initially, this presented an insurmountable technical difficulty. Du Pont Engineers considered it technologically impossible to cast this sculpture in this size in Lucite. Beasley subsequently purchased an autoclave and began to experiment with varying casting techniques. After 18 months, he had found the technological solution for making his transparent sculpture utilizing the correct relationship of heat and pressure during the polymerization of the acrylic. Initially, technicians had considered this impossible.[16] In 1970, his work "Apolymon" was finally presented to the public in Sacramento, and the response was very enthusiastic.[17] In an interview with Paul Mills,

Beasley explains, "This work was inspired by an artistic vision of something massive and clear that dramatizes the penetration of light and color." Mills adds, "Apolymon does precisely that with astonishing splendor. Daylight plunges onto the polished surface of the piece, then appears to float within its luminous mass and splinters to the surface in points of light with disjoined brilliance and color."[18]

In an interview with M. Donohue printed in this catalog, he pointed out that his decision to work with transparent materials once again confronted him with the problem that mass, volume and gravity influence one another. Beasley tries to create conditions in his works and find forms that challenge our visual patterns and experiences.

V.

In the 1970s, Beasley created an entire series of transparent sculptures using Lucite which are formally characterized by an association of organic forms, crystalline structures and tight stereometric bodies in the form of polyhedrons he combines with each other in the most diverse combinations. These works rely on their form which always seems to disappear and change due to the effect of light. This often makes it nearly impossible for the observer to clearly recognize the lines of the sculpture or to precisely define the front and back side of the work. In this context, he said to M. Donohue, "When you looked through those early early clear works, you had to acknowledge that surface was ambiguous and diffuse. As the piece reflected its ambient space and ambient light, as you looked through the piece, questions of where its mass began and ended were raised not in logical but in emotional ways"

Beasley developed the forms for his next phase of work from his transparent sculptures. At the onset of the 1980s, he had solved the aesthetic and technical problems of transparent sculpture and turned to new forms and materials. He now created steel sculptures by adding a basic module out of hexagonal, burnished, stainless steel that he combined to form space - enveloping bodies and structures. He first developed these hexagonal forms during the construction of molds for his transparent sculptures. They became

the primary basis of his work for the following years. He constructed hollow bodies that he combined to form dynamic structures in additive arrangements that frequently display a certain formal similarity with the big stabiles of Alexander Calder. It is characteristic of these often monumental pieces that have been described as "crystalline sculptures,"[19] that the arrangement of sculptural forms frequently appears to contradict our sense of gravity. A certain transparency connects them to the works of the 1970s. Unified bodies and open elements of the forms come about by joining individual elements to hollow bodies, permitting an integration of the surrounding space into the sculpture.

The burnished surface of the stainless steel reflects light and simultaneously captures the color of the surroundings, leading to an optical dissolution of the strict constructive structure of the work. One of these works, "Artemon," was on display in the "California Sculpture Show" in the Mannheim Kunsthalle in 1984 and 1985.[20]

VI.

The year 1987 marked the beginning of a new creative phase in Bruce Beasley's work. He was invited to an international steel sculpture symposium in Krefeld, Germany. He created a model out of cardboard—"Intersections"—that was built according to the artist's exact specification out of Cor-ten steel in Krefeld.[21]

This work represented a new phase in Beasley's work. Ever since, he has been making bronze sculptures that are formally determined by mingling cubic elements and unified stereometric bodies that expand on the space - enveloping structures of his previous works in steel. In addition, he has also been using a highly sophisticated computer program since 1988 to compose his sculptures. This enables him to draw on his previous sculptural experience to achieve completely new forms and it also gives him the opportunity to simultaneously develop his pieces from all sides using playful additions or fusions of cubic forms in order to achieve new, unexpected and surprising forms. It is very advantageous for him that he now has the opportunity to view the sculpture simultaneously from all sides on the monitor and to control its form with this method. In so doing, he opens new, creative dimensions that also offer the opportunity to react spontaneously to unexpected and innovative forms. He describes his working technique as drawing in a three dimensional space. This has given rise to Beasley's new, complex works with their descending or ascending shapes that intersect and seem to stay in a delicate balance. Beasley often works very long on a project until he finds the composition that harmonizes with his aesthetic and formal notions. "When I work at a computer," he says, "there is no front view, I am always working on the piece completely in the round at all times. New shapes that appear as a result of the new intersections go beyond my own previsualizations. A cube thrusting out of another cube is no longer a cube"[22]

Beasley has never begun his sculptures with drawings but always developed small models. Now, working on computers opens the way for him to fulfill his sculptural ideas much more quickly. The laborious creation of a model as a test vehicle for each sculptural idea is no longer necessary since he can fully understand the composition three - dimensionally on the computer monitor; the artist describes that as the biggest advantage of this method. As he said in an interview with M. Donohue, he was dissatisfied with the laborious creative process of his previous works and sought a method to make the models in a quick and spontaneous way. The computer enables him to test numerous variations of an idea on his monitor before building it. He compares working at a computer to drawing, the computer permitting him to experiment in three dimensional space such that he can work and find solutions for his sculptural problems more quickly.

When a form matches his idea, the individual elements are precisely transferred to foam core—a piece of polystyrene sandwiched between paper—using a plotter. This is the basis for an initial model which stays in his studio for an extended time to be certain that the composition is fully resolved before casting it in bronze. This procedure applies primarily to smaller works that Beasley has cast in bronze. Beasley chooses another process for his larger works. For this process, the individual components of the form are also trans-

ferred to foam core and used as patterns for bronze plates, which he then joins together as sculptures in a very technologically involved process in his studio. There are examples of his smaller works as well as the largest works made by joining bronze plates in the exhibit.

Beasley not only uses great care in the technically perfect execution of his sculptures but also in the treatment of the surface. He frequently applies carefully executed, highly differentiated textures or structures to achieve different surface effects, and he applies a patina to his works himself using very different color tones, shaded light or dark, and a color scale which may range from red to ocher, blue or green. For Beasley, the patina is an integrated component of his works. His distinctive works achieve their appeal to a large extent from color, used to specifically evoke certain emotional effects. Thus, Bruce Beasley is part of a characteristic tradition of California art that allots a great deal of attention to issues of surface.

The formal concepts for his works stem from different sources. Usually, it is a natural form, such as the large, unusual cliff formations of Monument Valley in Arizona, crystals, molecular structures or bones that stir his creative process. Based on the simplest stereometric bodies such as cubes, pillars, columns, spheres or discs, he creates his new sculptures with combinations and intersections that are either characterized by a block like, static unity or the quality of enveloping space in a dynamic manner that seems to defy gravity. The formal arrangement of the intersecting polyhedrons, revealing linear edges, gives the impression of a kaleidoscopic vision of shape.

Bruce Beasley's works are space - enveloping and space - defining. His engagement with spatial problems shows association with Eduardo Chillida's work, with whom he is a friend. Beasley would like to make space something that can be vigorously experienced and defined by mass and volume to create the impression of silence or movement. In his interview with M. Donohue, he explains at length that the emotional aspect of his work is especially important. He feels that the more he concentrates on the emotional expression of the forms, the better the sculpture turns out.

VII.

When summarizing Bruce Beasley's sculptural work, one can establish that he turns to new materials and new problems of form in cycles of approximately 10 years. In the 1960s, he worked with welded and cast iron, cast aluminum and industrial scrap; in the 1970s he worked with transparent materials; in the 1980s he constructed space-enveloping steel sculptures based on hexagonal forms that were then replaced with his cubical bronze sculptures developed with the aid of his computer. The latter sculptures are currently on view. These changes are always the result of an intellectual evolution and not just the result of a new formal point of origin or the challenge of new materials. One thing remains consistent: his works are the result of a methodological approach reminiscent of the approach of Abstract Expressionist artists, even if he has used the aid of a computer to conceptualize them. They also partake of the formal tradition of Constructivism and related artistic movements.

The origin of his sculptural form is often found in nature, be it crystalline shapes, fossils or bones he studies in order to understand how individual parts fit together to make a whole. By the same token, he constructs his sculptures out of individual elements in such a way that the whole appears unified. In an interview with M. Donohue he said, "There is a close parallel between success in nature and success in art. In both cases success is achieved when nothing can be added or removed"[23]

Manfred Fath

1. Cf. e.g. Jones, C.A. Bay Area Figurative Art, 1950-1965, Berkeley and Los Angeles 1990 - Joachimides, C.M. and Rosenthal, N. American Art in the 20th Century, Painting and Sculpture, Munich 1993 pp. 97 ff - Hopkins, H.T. California Painters: New York, San Francisco 1989

2. Catalog: American Sculpture of the Sixties, Los Angeles County Museum, Los Angeles, 1967.

3. Anderson, W., American Sculpture in Process, 1930/1970, New York, p.175.

4. Butterfield, J., Sculpture is Closer to Reality than Painting in: California Sculpture Show, Los Angeles, Bordeaux, Mannheim, West Bretton, Oslo, 1984/85, p.25.

5. Weiner, H., The Los Angeles School, in Catalog: 1972 - USA West Coast, Hamburg, Hannover, Cologne, Stuttgart, 1972, p.113.

6. Hopkins, p.10, Compare also Coplans, J., The New Sculpture and Technology, in: Catalog of American Sculpture of the Sixties, P.21 ff.

7. Weiner, op cit. p.114.

8. Heißenbüttel, H., West Coast and New Esthetics in: 1972 - USA West Coast, p.11.

9. Ibid. p.10.

10. Lippard, L., Catalog of California Sculpture Show, p.25.

11. Cf.: A Report on the Art and Technology Program of the Los Angeles County Museum 1967 - 1971, Los Angeles, 1971.

12. Heißenbüttel, op cit., p.11.

13. Gabo, N. and Pevsner, A., The Realist Manifesto, in: Naum Gabo, Sixty Years of Constructivism, Ed. Nash, ST. A and Merkert, J., Munich, 1986

14. Ibid.

15. Elsen, A.A., Bruce Beasley's Personal "Cubism": 1987-1990, in Catalog: Bruce Beasley, An Exhibition of Bronze Sculpture, 1990/1991, p.5.

16. Catalog: California Sculpture Show, p.66.

17. Ibid.

18. Ibid.

19. Catalog: California Sculpture Show, p.37.

20. Catalog, California Sculpture Show, Fig. p.63.

21. Catalog: Krefeld.

22. Cf. Fath, M., "The only reason for my being an artist is my joy in discovering that I can create new forms," in: Catalog: Bruce Beasely, Bad Homburg 1993

23. Donohue, M., An Interview with Bruce Beasley, see subsequent interview in this catalog.

Bruce Beasley

André Malraux, damaliger Kultusminister von Frankreich, suchte persönlich auf der Pariser Biennale 1963 eine Skulptur von Bruce Beasley für die Sammlung des Musée d´Art Moderne in Paris aus. Die amerikanische Sektion und der Katalog wurden betreut von dem inzwischen verstorbenen Herschel B. Chipp, Professor für Moderne Kunst an der Universität von Kalifornien, Berkeley, der nur Werke von Bildhauern aussuchte, die in Berkeley studiert hatten. Im Katalog begründete er diese Auswahl: *"... presents for the judgement of an intentional audience a unique idea: sculpure having its origin in a university community. "*[1] Während in Europa Kunst schon immer an den Akademien gelehrt wurde, kam in Amerika die Ausübung der Kunst schon vor dem 2.Weltkrieg an die Universitäten, aber an keiner anderen Hochschule gelangte die Bildhauerei zu so großem Ansehen wie in Berkeley, wo Beasley sich 1959 als Student einschrieb.

Unter den renommierten Bildhauern, die in Berkeley lehrten, waren Jacques Schnier, bekannt für seine modernen gegenständlichen Skulpturen, kompakte kubistische Konstruktionen aus Holz und verschiedenen Metallen, und Richard O´Hanlon, ein Meister der Bildhauerei in Stein, der organische und geometrische Formen verschmolz, die manchmal an Henry Moore erinnerten. Die Technik des Schweißens führte Wilfred Zogbaum ein, der in Berkeley 1957 / 58 lehrte und Anfang der sechziger Jahre erneut dorthin berufen wurde. Zogbaum schuf ebenso wie seine Freunde David Smith und Hebert Ferber "Zeichnungen im Raum" und faßte die Materialien oft farbig; manchmal fügte er glatte Steine zu seinen Assemblagen hinzu. 1958 kam Sidney Gordin zur Fakultät; er hatte sich in New York einen Namen gemacht mit seinen Rechteck-Konstruktionen aus Metall, zu denen er von Mondrian und de Stijl inspiriert wurde. Ein Jahr später konnte Peter Voulkos gewonnen werden, der viel Leben in die Fakultät brachte. Mit seinen unsymmetrischen und nicht mehr funktionsbezogenen Töpfen, mit denen er der Formensprache der abstrakten expressionistischen Bilder folgte, die er bewunderte, erhob er das Medium Keramik aus dem Handwerklichen zur Kunstform. Harold Paris kam 1960 mit grundlegendem Wissen in pointiert expressionistischer Grafik, Erfahrung im Bronzeguß und ungewöhnlicher Energie. Zur gleichen Zeit wurde Donald Haskin nach Berkeley berufen. Er hatte in Minnesota eine Bronzegießerei betrieben und sollte an der Universität eine Gießerei einrichten. Zu diesem Vorhaben stießen auch Voulkos, Paris und Julius Schmidt, ein Gast-Bildhauer von der Cranbrook Academy in Michigan, an der er an einer sehr individuellen Form der Eisenskulptur gearbeitet hatte. Die Gießerei, "Garbanzo Works", wurde eine lebendige und aufregende Experimental-Werkstatt nahe dem Berkeley campus.

Schon während der Studienzeit und noch bevor Beasley seine eigenen Arbeiten in der Gießerei goß, hatte er Skulpturen aus Metallschrott zusammengebaut. Eines dieser Werke, *Lemures*, gewann einen Preis im San Francisco Annual, juriert von Dorothy Miller, der bekannten Kuratorin des New York Museum of Modern Art, die dann auch Beasleys Arbeit *Chorus* kaufte, als sie sie auf einer Ausstellung in der Everett Ellin Gallery in Los Angeles sah. Ein ähnliches Stück, *Tree House*, ebenfalls aus dem Jahr 1960, aus gußeisernen Abzugsrohren gefertigt, kam 1961 in die Bill Seitz *Art of Assemblage* - Ausstellung im Museum of Modern Art.

Diese Arbeiten, die ihren Ursprung in der städtischen Schrottkultur hatten, und die auch deren Sprache sprachen, erinnerten noch an die Stahl- und Eisenassemblagen von Richard Stankiewicz. Für Beasley waren sie auf Dauer zu sehr von dem abhängig, was man auf den Schrottplätzen vorfand. Er wollte lieber seine eigenen Formen schaffen. Er machte Skulpturen aus Styropor und goß dann seine selbstgeschaffenen Formen in Bronze und Aluminium in der Gießerei, die er in seinem Atelier eingerichtet hatte. *Icarus*, das Werk auf der Biennale in Paris, war in Aluminium gegossen. Es ist eine wunderbare, in die Höhe strebende Arbeit, die mit anmutiger Eleganz buchstäblich den Raum erobert. A. Malraux beschrieb sie als eine *"linear construction embracing but not filling the space, which it dominates."*[2] Es war nur folgerichtig, daß Beasley den Preis gewann: Vier Jahre zuvor, als ich Kommissar für die amerikanische Sektion der ersten Biennale des Jeunes in Paris gewesen war, hatte Beasleys Lehrer Peter Voulkos den Rodin-Preis gewonnen.

Ebenfalls 1963 erwarb das Guggenheim Museum Beasleys *Prometheus II* von 1963, eine innovative Arbeit, die sich an einer vertikalen Achse orientiert und mit einem langen Arm endet, der mit einer in die Höhe reichenden Klaue abschließt. Bruce Beasley war erst vierundzwanzig und arbeitete erst seit kurzem als Bildhauer, und doch waren seine Arbeiten sehr professionell und hatten ihren eigenen Charakter. Aber eigentlich hatte er mit Metall schon gearbeitet, als er noch die High School besuchte. 1939 in Los Angeles geboren, begann er, mit großer Leichtigkeit mit Metall zu arbeiten und bekam einen nationalen Preis für seine Arbeit. Er war auch sehr geschickt darin, Autos zu "Heißen Öfen" umzubauen, was seine Eltern wohl kaum fördern wollten, als sie ihren begabten Sohn auf das Dartmouth College schickten, wo er eine liberale Erziehung genoß. Dort entdeckte er Bildhauerei als Beruf. Er wechselte nach Berkeley, um in dieser anregenden Umgebung das Fach zu studieren.

Die meisterhaften Formen der Bildhauerei und Malerei eines David Smith und Franz Kline - zweier großer amerikanischer Künstler - bewunderte er, als er selbst an einer Serie in gegossenem Aluminium zu arbeiten begann, in der sich Stärke mit Eleganz paarte. In der Tat beinhaltet eine Arbeit wie *Icarus* jenes bildhauerische Gespür für Präzision, Offenheit der Konstruktion und des Im-Raum-Zeichnens, wie es beispielsweise für David Smith gilt. Es besteht auch Bezug zu der direkten Gestik in Klines Malerei mit ihren mächtigen Kreisen, Bögen und Pinselhieben. In der Besprechung von Beasleys Ausstellung in Los Angeles 1963 schrieb Henry Seldis, Kritiker der *Los Angeles Times* : *"Bruce Beasley, a San Francisco artist in his early twenties, is the sort of rare precocious talent that achieves mastery of content and technique at a remarkable early state in a more than promising career."*[3]

Nachdem er diese Technik beherrschte, genügte es Beasley nicht mehr, Skulpturen in Aluminium zu gießen. Gegen Ende der 60er Jahre wollte er über die Möglichkeiten der Metallskulptur hinausgelangen. Er träumte davon, transparente Skulpturen zu machen, Arbeiten, bei denen eine Vielzahl von Ansichten - vorn, hinten, seitlich - gleichzeitig vom Bildhauer und vom Betrachter gesehen werden konnten. Er erwog,

Skulpturen aus Glas zu machen, aber verwarf diesen Gedanken wieder, da ihm Glas zu schwer und zu spröde war. Um Skulpturen voller Klarheit und Reinheit zu schaffen, verwandte er Acryl. Als das Land Kalifornien für eine große öffentliche Skulptur, die in der Landeshauptstadt installiert werden sollte, einen 50,000-Dollar-Wettbewerb ausschrieb, reichte Beasley eine Maquette aus Lucite ein und bekam den Auftrag.

Damals wußte er noch nicht, wie man eine sehr große Arbeit in Acryl gießt. Sein Modell, 15 cm tief, sollte als fertige Skulptur 120 cm tief sein. Der Künstler befand sich in einem Dilemma: Da ihm technisches Wissen und Ausrüstung fehlten, wandte er sich an das Chemiewerk DuPont, Hersteller von Acrylharz unter dem Markennamen Lucite. Das Material wurde ihm gestellt, aber die Fachleute meinten, ein Werk von solch monumentaler Größe sei nicht machbar. Beharrlich arbeitete Beasley fast anderthalb Jahre nach dem Motto "trial and error" an dem Projekt. Er mußte eine neue Gußmethode entwickeln und dazu benötigte er einen großen Druckofen, Autoklav genannt, mit exakter Temperatur- und Druckkontrolle für den Wechsel des Acryls vom flüssigen in den festen Zustand. Als Glücksbringer für diesen scheinbar alchemistischen Prozeß verzierte er den Autoklaven mit Ornamenten der Indianer aus dem Nordwesten, wie er sie aus seiner Sammlung von Eingeborenen-Kunst aus Britisch-Kolumbien in seinem Haus in Oakland kannte. Für die Ingenieure von DuPont war dies eine überflüssige Dekoration; aber schließlich mußten sie akzeptieren, daß sie nie zu den gleichen Ergebnissen gelangt wären. Als der Trocknungsvorgang beendet war, war das Werk vollendet. Nach einem langen Prozeß sorgfältigen Polierens wurde *Apolymon* auf dem Areal des California State Capitol aufgestellt und fand begeisterte Zustimmung sowohl in der Öffentlichkeit als auch bei den Kritikern. Mit seinen Maßen von 4,50 x 1,20 x 2,40 m und einem Gewicht von etwa 6 Tonnen war es die bis dahin größte gegossene Konstruktion aus Acryl. Aber es war viel mehr als ein technisches Meisterstück: Die erste moderne Skulptur, die der Staat Kalifornien in Auftrag gegeben hatte, war ein großes bedeutendes Kunstwerk. Die zugrundeliegende Symmetrie der leuchtenden Skulptur wird durch viele Variationen unterbrochen. Die schwingenartigen Arme erzeugen dynamische Stöße und Gegenstöße. Das plastische

Äußere umfaßt Höhlungen, Grate, Spalten und viele Faltungen. Die leuchtende Klarheit reagiert auf Licht und so glitzert und funkelt *Apolymon* unter der kalifornischen Sonne und erscheint ruhig, wenn der Himmel bewölkt ist.

Apolymon und die vielen anderen Werke aus Lucite, mit denen der Bildhauer sich in den folgenden zehn Jahren beschäftigte, kann man betrachten als Fortsetzung der konstruktivistischen Tradition, deren er sich sehr wohl bewußt war. In ihrem sog. *Realistischen* (eigentlich konstruktivistischen) *Manifest* erklärten Naum Gabo und Antoine Pevsner ihr Ablehnen von Masse als Element von Skulptur. Unter Punkt 4 des Manifestes tadelten sie: *"We renounce in sculpture, the mass as a sculptural element... You sculptors of all shades and direction, still adhere to the age-old prejudice that you cannot free the volume from mass. We take four planes and we construct with them the same volume as of four tons of mass."*[4]

Besonders Gabo machte in seinem Werk eine neue Art von Raum in der Skulptur zugänglich. Für seine Arbeiten verwendete er alle möglichen Arten verfügbaren transparenten Materials wie Glas, Kunststoff, Zelluloid und Perspex, um die Transparenz deutlich zu machen und um den inneren Raum der Skulptur sichtbar werden zu lassen. Auch László Moholy-Nagy, der in den 40er Jahren in Chicago arbeitete, suchte nach einer Lösung, um sein Konzept von Raum/Zeit in drei Dimensionen auszudrücken. Er war der Überzeugung, daß Licht ebenso wie Ton oder Stein ein Medium der Bildhauerei sein könne, und er schuf Arbeiten, die er als "Raum-Modulatoren" bezeichnete. In seinem Buch *"Vision in Motion"*, das seine Intelligenz und Vorstellungskraft zum Ausdruck bringt, schreibt er zur Illustration eines rhomboiden Raum-Modulators aus Plexiglas: *"Transparent plastic molded or shaped by hand is a new enrichment of contemporary sculpture. Though we have had transparent material for ages - glass - its handling was rather difficult. There have been very few important glass sculptures. Thermoplastics can be handled more easily than glass; they can be bend, warped, rolled and cut."*[5]

Beasleys Arbeit, in der sich das Intuitive mit dem Wissenschaftlichen verbindet, gehört ganz deutlich in diese Tradition moderner Skulptur. Nach einer monumentalen Arbeit für Sacramento werden seine Skulpturen aus Lucite in Form und Krümmung einfacher, möglicherweise eine Reaktion auf die geometrischen Formen der Minimal Art in New York und die geometrischen "Fetish Finish" - Skulpturen in Los Angeles. Aber selbst wenn in Beasleys Acrylarbeiten die Hauptform zu einem Würfel reduziert ist, belebt die Spiegelung auf der Oberfläche die Form und unterscheidet so sein Werk von der absichtsvollen Abgeschlossenheit der Formen von Tony Smith, Donald Judd oder Dewain Valentine.

Die tiefe Kluft zwischen humanistischer und naturwissenschaftlicher Haltung verneinend, die C.P. Snow gegen Ende der 50er Jahre aufgezeichnet hatte, zieht Beasley in einem Artikel über sein Werkschaffen im *Science Magazine* Parallelen zwischen den Disziplinen: Wenn man Schritt für Schritt logisch von A nach B geht, kommt man nicht sehr weit. Man erreicht eine Wand, über die man nicht steigen kann. Und dann hilft einem die Intuition, und zwar in einer Intensität, die man nicht für möglich gehalten hätte. Was da mit der Acryl-Technik geschehen ist, dieser Prozeß unterscheidet sich nicht so sehr von der Kunst. In der Kunst kommt das Bild durch die Intuition - man kommt dahin, wo man vorher noch nicht war. Aber wenn man dort ist, ist der Weg klarer. Sowohl in der Wissenschaft als auch in der Kunst ist der einfache Ansporn: Forschen macht Spaß."[6]

Der wissenschaftliche Aspekt seiner Arbeit wird auch 1976 in der Zusammenarbeit mit Ozeanographen zur Entwicklung einer Tiefsee-Taucherkugel aus Acryl deutlich; in diesem Zusammenhang ist zu sehen, daß Beasley von Jugend an ein Scuba-Taucher war. Das Ergebnis wurde erstmals im Exploratorium in San Francisco ausgestellt, einem Museum, das von dem Physiker Frank Oppenheimer gegründet worden war, um Wissenschaft und Kunst einander begegnen zu lassen. Die 2000 Pfund schwere und etwa 1,85 m große Kugel kann bis zu einer Tiefe von ca. 3000 m verwendet werden. Er arbeitete zusammen mit Dr. J. Stachiw vom Naval Undersea Center in San Diego. Dr. Stachiw entwickelte die mechanischen Teile, während Beasley die riesige Kugel goß. Das Gerät wurde u.a. eingesetzt bei der Unterwassersuche nach den Leichen der Männer und der Frau, die bei der Explo-

sion des Challenger-Raumschiffes 1986 ums Leben gekommen waren. Ein Anerkennungsschreiben der National Space Agency hängt seit der Zeit in Bruce Beasleys Atelier. Die Taucherkugel kann man auch als groß dimensionierte minimalistische Skulptur betrachten.

Als der Bildhauer sich die technischen und ästhetischen Bedingungen transparenter Skulptur zu eigen gemacht hatte, verlangten seine Ideen nach neuen Formen und Materialien. Er bekam Aufträge für sechs große Skulpturen, unter anderem für den Campus der Universität von Stanford, die Stadt Anchorage, die Flughäfen von San Francisco und Miami und für die Djerassi Foundation in Woodside, Kalifornien, die er nun in Edelstahl ausführte. Es entstanden monumentale Skulpturen, aus großen hexagonalen, auf Hochglanz polierten Facetten zusammengeschweißt. Diese sorgfältig gearbeiteten Skulpturen stehen auf spitzen Standpunkten, von denen aus sie zu beachtlicher Höhe aufragen. In den offenen Strukturen wechseln Leerräume mit festen Polyedern. Der Betrachter, der durch die Skulptur oder um sie herum geht, entdeckt ständig wechselnde räumliche Muster. Wie Calders Stabiles scheinen diese Skulpturen architektonische Environments zu suggerieren. Die Hochglanz-Politur auf den Flächen von Beasleys Skulpturen spiegelt darüber hinaus auch Himmel und Landschaft und ermöglicht so eine visuelle Erfahrung, die das Umfeld der Skulptur mit einbezieht.

Die Bronzeplastik, Thema dieser Ausstellung, ist seit 1987, als er zum Internationalen Skulpturen-Symposium in Krefeld eingeladen worden war, zentrales Anliegen seines Œuvres. Ein Pappmodell seiner Arbeit *Intersections*, 1987, wurde im Rahmen des Symposiums exakt in 5facher Vergrößerung als Skulptur aus Cor-ten-Stahl ausgeführt; die glatten Oberflächen und scharfen Kanten des Originals wurden dabei beibehalten. Beasley, der sich schon immer sehr für Kristallografie interessiert hatte, nannte das Werk *Titiopoli´s Arch*, eine Hommage an den ehemaligen Studenten dieser Wissenschaft in Griechenland. Die Vergrößerung eröffnete ihm die Möglichkeiten, sich mit seiner Arbeit in eine neue Richtung zu bewegen. 1988 begann er mit Bronzegüssen. Wieder fand er einen Weg, Kunst und Technik zu verbinden. Seit fünf Jahren benutzt er zur Entwicklung seiner Skulpturen den Computer als Zeichenbrett. Der Einsatz eines hochentwickelten Computers macht es ihm möglich, eine kontinuierliche Veränderung von Formen unmittelbar zu visualisieren. Als er noch mit Lucite arbeitete, lag sein Anliegen darin, mehrere Ansichten durch Transparenz gleichzeitig zu vergegenwärtigen. Jetzt ermöglicht es ihm der Computer, das Werk fast gleichzeitig von allen Seiten zusammenzusetzen; ein Tastendruck läßt neue Kuben oder Winkel entstehen. Selbst bei den frühen Assemblagen aus Fundstücken, kümmerte er sich wenig um den Eindruck der handwerklich-technischen Umsetzung. Wie die Konzeptkünstler, und wie vielleicht viele gute Künstler im Laufe der Geschichte, legt Beasley mehr Wert auf intellektuelle als auf handwerkliche Fertigkeiten. Aber jetzt kann er seine Komponenten auf dem Computer selbst erschaffen, anstatt im Industrieschrott danach zu suchen.

Beasley benutzt einen hochspezialisierten Hewlett Packard Computer, der ihm vom Hersteller für seine Experimente geschenkt wurde. Er spielt mit unterschiedlichen Formen, fügt sie hinzu, nimmt sie weg, kippt und bewegt sie mit großer Geschwindigkeit, läßt sie einander durchdringen und schafft so interessante Interaktionen zwischen den Formen.

So experimentiert er einige Tage lang, bis er mit der Form, die auf dem Ausdruck erscheint, gestalterisch zufrieden ist. Per Computer wird sie dann zu planen, zweidimensionalen Mustern transformiert, die als numerierte Teile, dreidimensional und aus verschiedenen Blickwinkeln projiziert, vom Künstler in einem Buch zusammengefaßt werden. Es wird benutzt für die Konstruktion eines Pappmodells. Bis dahin ist es noch möglich, mit dem Computer Veränderungen vorzunehmen. Schließlich werden diese Vorlagen auf einen geschäumten Kern aus Polyester und Papier aufgebracht. Die Gießerei in Berkeley schmilzt den Schaumstoffkern heraus und gießt Bronze in die entstandenen Hohlräume. So entsteht die plastische Form, die dann durch Säure patiniert wird. Die Patina kann hell oder dunkel sein, einen warmen orange-goldenen Ton haben oder einen kalten blaugrünen. Oft wird durch grafische Elemente, die der Künstler in den Schaumkern geritzt hat, die Oberfläche zusätzlich strukturiert.

Kuben, Scheiben, Schäfte, Kugeln, trapezoide sowie säulenartige Formen und faszinierende Schnittstellen, das beinhaltet das reiche Vokabular dieser authentischen Werke Beasleys. Wichtige Anregungen für seine Werke schöpft der Künstler aus frühen Erinnerungen an die Bergstümpfe des Monument Valley in Arizona, einer einzigartigen und wahrhaft atemberaubenden Landschaft mit ihrer Weite und ihren unglaublichen Felsformationen. Diese Erinnerungen spiegeln sich wider in Arbeiten wie *Mesa*, 1992, und *Refuge*, 1993. Beasley spricht auch von den Bauelementen natürlicher Formen als Quelle für seine Arbeit, von Kristallen, Knochen und von Molekularstrukturen. Erwähnt sei in diesem Zusammenhang seine umfangreiche Sammlung von Tierschädeln aller Art in seinem Atelier.

Intersection, die erste Arbeit dieser Serie, besteht aus durcheinandergewürfelten Kuben, die - von einer Strebe gehalten - in den Raum ragen. Ein ähnliches Schweben der sich durchdringenden Formen erscheint in *Bateleur*, 1989, aber diesmal stößt eine Form - sie suggeriert das Volumen eines virtuellen Kreises -, die an einen umgekehrten Obelisken erinnert, steil nach unten und hält in verblüffender Weise Balance. Bei *Apparition* aus dem gleichen Jahr sammelt sich eine große Zahl unterschiedlicher Kuben am oberen Ende eines schräg aufragenden Armes. Variationen zu diesem Thema erscheinen in *Thrust*, 1991, und *Breakout*, 1991. Schließlich gibt es Arbeiten wie *Precursor*, 1992, in der kubische Formen zu Massen verdichtet sind, die sich an den Boden, auf dem sie liegen, zu schmiegen scheinen. Das sehr ähnliche *Uplift* II, 1992, vermittelt ein Gefühl des Ansteigens, wie das auch im Titel zum Ausdruck kommt.

Haben die früheren Arbeiten Namen aus der griechischen Mythologie getragen, so orientieren sich die Titel jetzt bei den jüngeren Arbeiten an der Bewegung der Formerscheinung, so zum Beispiel *Ceremony*, 1989, mit seiner bewußt gebrochenen säulenhaften Struktur, oder *Spokesman*, 1993, bei dem ein sehr gewichtiges Oberteil von einem relativ kleinen Schaft getragen wird, was beim Betrachter Erstaunen über die gewagte Balance auslöst. *Pillars of Cypress*, 1990, ein rechteckiger Schaft mit abfallenden Blöcken, erhielt seinen Titel in Erinnerung an die Katastrophe des Loma Prieta Erdbebens 1989 und seiner Opfer beim Einsturz eines Abschnittes des Cypress Freeways. Beasley hatte über dreißig Jahre in der Nähe des Unglücksortes gelebt und gearbeitet. Sein Sohn und er halfen bei den Rettungsarbeiten. Mit der Arbeit thematisiert er die Stärke der Mitmenschen, die den Opfern auf dem zerstörten Freeway zu Hilfe kamen, wenn er erklärt: "It symbolizes the pillars of the neighborhood that stood when the pillars of the freeway failed."[7] Dieser quadratischen Säule folgten eine Reihe verwandter Strukturen wie *Sentinel*, 1990, *Tower of Silence,* 1991, und *Watchtower*, 1992, wohl die eleganteste dieser Arbeiten. Bei *Ascender*, 1991, sind zwei gestreckte senkrechte Schäfte im oberen Teil durch einen horizontalen Querbalken verbunden. Die Arbeit ist etwa 1,60 m hoch, aber man kann sie sich in monumentalem Maßstab vorstellen als eine Art Triumphbogenarchitektur. In der Tat gibt es eine Reihe von Entwürfen, deren Ausführung wegen ihrer Größe nicht mehr im Gußverfahren möglich ist. Diese Arbeiten werden in Beasleys Atelier aus riesigen Bronzeplatten zusammengefügt, die geschnitten und mit unsichtbaren Nähten zusammengeschweißt werden. Die visuelle Wirkung der linearen, scharf ausgeführten Kanten und die technische Perfektion bei der Herstellung bestimmen das ästhetische Erleben dieser Arbeiten.

Wie schon seine früheren Arbeiten manifestieren Beasleys neue Bronzen einen Synergismus von Kunst und Wissenschaft. Diese Polyeder sind gefertigt mit der klaren Präzision des industriellen Zeitalters: sie sind entworfen mit Hilfe von postindustriellen Computern. Die Analyse ihrer Entstehung aber vergegenwärtigt sie als das Ergebnis der Vision des Künstlers.

In letzter Zeit beschäftigt sich Bruce Beasley mit Spielen wie Hermann Hesses Magister Ludi. Neuerdings entstehen auf dem Computer Zeichnungen, in denen gekippte Perspektiven und sich überschneidende Flächen unerwartete Schatten werfen, die uns an die scharfen und geheimnisvollen Schatten in De Chiricos metaphysischen Bildern erinnern. Wie die Skulpturen, die er über einen Zeitraum von mehr als dreißig Jahren geschaffen hat, sprechen auch diese Zeichnungen sowohl unseren Verstand als auch unser Gefühl an.

Peter Selz
Berkeley, Sommer 1993

Anmerkungen

1. Herschel B. Chipp, "Introduction", *Onze Sculpteurs Americaine,* Berkeley, University Art Gallery, 1964. O.S.
   Außer Beasley erhielten einige andere Künstler Anerkennung für wichtige Arbeit. Unter ihnen waren James Melchert, Charles Ross und Stephen de Staebler.

2. André Malraux, zit. nach "A French Honor", *San Francisco Chronicle,* 4. Februar 1964

3. Henry Seldis, "Young Sculptor Displays Rare, Precocious Talent", *Los Angeles Times*, 3.Juni 1963

4. Gabo und Pevsner, "Das realistische Manifest", in Herschel B.Chipp, Peter Selz und Joshua C. Taylor, *Theories of Modern Art,* Berkeley, The University of California Press, 1968, S.329

5. L. Moholy-Nagy, *Vision in Motion,* Chicago, Paul Theobald, 1947, S.235

6. Bruce Beasley in Michael Rogers, "The Sculpture Transparent", *Science*, Bd.4, Nr.10, (Dezember 1983), S.45

7. Beasley in Janet Kornblum, "Out of the Rubble", *The Times-Star,* Oakland, 2. Mai 1990

Bruce Beasley

Andre Malraux, Minister for Cultural Affairs of France at the time, personally selected a sculpture by Bruce Beasley for the permanent collection of the Paris Musee d'Art Moderne from the Paris Biennale in 1963. The American segment, and its catalog *Onze Sculpteurs Americain* were under the direction of the late Herschel B. Chipp, who was professor of modern art at the University of California, Berkeley. He chose works only by sculptors who had studied at the Berkeley campus, writing in the catalogue that this selection "presents for the judgement of an intentional audience a unique idea: sculpture having its origin in a university community".[1] Whereas in Europe art is taught at the academies, the practice of art entered the universities in America prior to World War II, but there was no other school in which the pursuit of sculpture flourished as much as at Berkeley, where Beasley enrolled as a student in 1959.

Among the distinguished group of sculptors teaching at Berkeley were Jacques Schnier, who was well known for his modernist figurative sculptures and had turned to compact cubist constructions made of wood and various metals, Richard O'Hanlon, a master stone carver, who fused organic and geometric shapes in fine works which at times would recall Henry Moore. The technique of direct welded metal was introduced by Wilfred Zogbaum who taught at Berkeley from 1957 to 1958 and was invited back in the early '60s. Zogbaum, like his friends David Smith, and Herbert Ferber made "drawings in space" and used materials which he often painted, sometimes adding smooth stones to his assemblages. In 1958 Sidney Gordin, who had also established a reputation in New York for his metal constructions of rectangles, inspired by Mondrian and de Stijl, joined the faculty. Then, a year later Peter Voulkos was recruited and brought great vitality to the department. When Voulkos made pots that were no longer symmetrical or utilitarian, but were put together like the Abstract Expressionist paintings he admired, the medium of ceramics was permanently altered from a craft to an art form. Harold Paris arrived in 1960 with a background in poignant Expressionist graphics, experience in bronze casting and extraordinary energy and visual culture. At the same time Donald Haskin, who had actually operated a bronze foundry in Minnesota was asked to come to Berkeley to start a foundry at the university and was joined in this enterprise by Voulkos, and Paris as well as Julius Schmidt, a visiting sculptor from the Cranbrook Academy in Michigan, where he had done some highly personal iron sculpture. The foundry which was called Garbanzo Works became a vital and exciting experimental workshop near the Berkeley Campus.

Before casting his own work at the foundry and while still a student, Beasley had made sculpture assembled from pieces of discarded metal. One of them *Lemures* was awarded a prize in the San Francisco Annual which was juried by Dorothy Miller, the famed curator of New York's Museum of Modern Art who then acquired Beasley's piece *Chorus* when she saw it on exhibition at Everett Ellin Gallery in Los Angeles. A similar work, *Tree House*, also from 1960 and made of scraps of cast-iron sewer pipe was included in Bill Seitz's *Art of Assemblage* exhibition at MoMA in 1961.

These works, originating from the urban junk culture and expressing its vernacular were still reminiscent of the steel and iron assemblages by Richard Stankiewicz and were, for Beasley too dependent on whatever could be found in the junk yards. He wanted, rather, to create his own forms and did so when he made sculpture from Styrofoam and then cast his own forms into bronze and aluminum at a foundry he had built at his studio. *Icarus*, the piece in the Paris Biennale was cast in aluminum. It is a wonderful, soaring work which literally sweeps into space with graceful elegance. A. Malraux described it as a "linear construction embracing but not filling the space, which it dominates".[2] There was also a certain consonance in Beasley's receiving the award: Four years earlier, when I was the commissioner for the American section of the first Paris Biennale de Jeunes, it was Beasley's teacher, Peter Voulkos who received the Rodin Prize. It was also in 1963 that the Guggenheim Museum acquired Beasley's *Prometheus II* (1963), a highly inventive work, tightly designed along a vertical axis with a long arm ending in a talon reaching into the sky. Bruce Beasley was only twenty four and had

been making sculpture for a very short time and was already doing work of a highly professional and authentic nature. But, actually, he had been working in metal since he was in high school. Born in Los Angeles in 1939, he began working with metal with great ease and received a national prize for his shop work. He was also adept at converting automobiles into hot rods, which was hardly what his family had in mind for their gifted son. He went to Dartmouth College to get a liberal education and while there, discovered that sculpture could be a profession and transferred to Berkeley to study sculpture in this fertile environment.

At the time of the Paris Biennale, when he began working on a series of cast aluminum pieces which combined strength with elegance he admired the work of two major American artists. David Smith and Franz Kline for their mastery of shapes, be it in sculpture or painting. In fact, a work such as *Icarus* shares the openness of construction, the drawing-in-space element of David Smith as well as the sculptor's sense of precision. It also relates to the directness of gesture in Kline's paintings and their powerful loops, arcs, and thrusts. Reviewing Beasley's 1963 exhibition in Los Angeles, Henry Seldis, the critic of the *Los Angeles Times* commented that "Bruce Beasley, a San Francisco artist in his early twenties, is the sort of rare precocious talent that achieves mastery of content and technique at a remarkable early state in a more than promising career."[3]

But Beasley was not satisfied with making cast aluminum sculpture, once he had mastered that medium.

By the late 1960s Beasley wanted to go beyond the possibilities provided by metal sculpture. He dreamt of making transparent sculpture, work in which multiple views — front, back, sides, could be seen simultaneously by the sculptor and the observer. He thought of making sculpture out of glass, but discarded that material as being too heavy and too inflexible and turned to acrylic to make sculpture of clarity and purity. When the State of California announced a $50,000 competition for a major public sculpture to be set up in the state capitol, Beasley submitted a Lucite maquette and was awarded the commission.

At that time, he did not yet know how to cast an enormous work in acrylic. His model was 6 inches thick — the finished sculpture called for a thickness of 4 feet. The artist was indeed in a quandary: He lacked the engineering knowledge and he lacked the equipment. He approached DuPont chemical, manufacturers of Lucite, their brand name for acrylic resin. They eventually donated the material to Beasley but their experts informed him that a work of such monumental scale could not be done. Beasley, however, persisted and worked by trial and error for about eighteen months on this project. He had to invent a new casting process which involved a huge pressure oven, called an autoclave as well as precise temperature and pressure controls for the transformation of the liquid acrylic to its solid state of pure transparency. For good luck in this seemingly alchemical process he decorated the autoclave with a Northwest Indian design, not very different from the fine collection of indigenous art from British Columbia in his Oakland house. Du Pont engineers would never have made such a useless design and acknowledged they could not have achieved the same results. When the curing was completed, the work turned out with perfection.

Then, after a long process of careful polishing *Apolymon* was installed on the grounds of California's state capitol and greeted with enthusiasm by the public and critics alike. Fifteen feet long, four feet deep and eight feet high and weighing about six tons, it was the largest construction of acrylic plastic ever cast. But it was much more than a technical feat: This, the first modern sculpture ever commissioned by the State of California, was a major work of art. The basic symmetry of the luminous sculpture is broken up by many variations. Its wing-like arms create dynamic thrusts and counter-thrusts. Its pure plastic finish embraces hollows, ridges, crevices and many folds. Its brilliant clarity responds to light and *Apolymon,* reflecting light, sparkles in the California sun, while appearing placid on a cloudy day. *Apolymon* and the many other Lucite pieces which occupied the sculptor for another ten years or so, can be seen as a continuation of the Constructivst tradition, of which he was well aware. In their so called *Realist* (actually Constructivist) *Manifesto* Naum Gabo and Antoine Pevsner proclaimed their repudiation of mass as a sculptural element. They reproved traditional sculpture, saying in the 4th Precept of the Manifesto: "We renounce in sculpture, the mass as a sculptural element ... You sculptors of all shades and direction, still adhere to the age-old prejudice that you cannot free the volume from mass. We take four planes and we construct with them the same volume as of four tons of mass". [4]

It was Gabo, especially, whose work celebrated a new sense of space in sculpture. In his sculptures he used all sorts of transparent materials, glass and available synthetics such as celluloid and perspex to affirm transparency and to reveal interior space. Similarly, L.Moholy-Nagy, working in Chicago in the 1940s sought a solution to articulate his concept of space/ time in three dimensions. Convinced that light itself, like clay or stone, could be a medium in sculpture, he constructed works that he called "space-modulators". In his book *Vision in Motion* which summarized his intelligence and imagination, he captions the illustration of one Plexiglass and rhomboid space modulator by writing: "Transparent plastic molded or shaped by hand is a new enrichment of contemporary sculpture. Though we have had transparent material for ages - glass - its handling was rather difficult. There have been very few important glass sculptures. Thermoplastics can be handled more easily than glass; they can be bent, warped, rolled and cut." [5]

Beasley's work, combining the intuitive with the scientific, clearly belongs to this tradition of modernist sculpture. Subsequent to his monumental piece for Sacramento, his Lucite sculptures become simplified in shape and curvature, possibly in response to the geometric shapes of Minimal Sculpture in New York and the practitioners of geometric sculptures with "fetish finish" in Los Angeles. But even when the principal shape is reduced to a cube in Beasley's acrylic works, the centicular reflection enlivens the form and differentiates his work from the deliberate hermeticism of the simplified gestalts by Tony Smith, Donald Judd or Dewain Valentine.

Denying the deep cleavage between the humanistic and scientific cultures announced by C.P. Snow in the late 1950s, Beasley draws parallels between the disciplines in an article about his work in *Science* magazine.

"Step by step logic, going from A to B can someties only take you so far. You arrive at a wall you can't climb over. And that's when intuition can take you over, to a point that you thought wasn't possible. That's what happened with the development of the acrylic technology. And I don't find that thought process so different from art. In art, intuition gives you the image — it takes you somewhere you haven't been before. But once you're there, the road is clearer. The motive, in both science and art is simple: Exploration is exhilarating." [6]

Pursuing the scientific aspect of his work, Beasley, a scuba diver since his youth worked with oceanographers to develop a transparent Bathysphere out of acrylic in 1976. It was first exhibited at the Exploratorium in San Francisco, a wondrous museum, committed to the meeting of art and science by its founder, the physicist Frank Oppenheimer. The 2000 pound 66 inch sphere could be used to a depth of 9,000 feet. Working with Dr. J. Stachiw of the Naval Undersea Center in San Diego who designed the mechanical parts, Beasley cast this huge globe which found an important application in the undersea search for the bodies of the men and woman who were killed in the explosion of the Challenger spacecraft in 1986 and a commendation from the National Space Agency to Bruce Beasley now hangs in his studio. The globe can also be seen as a piece of minimal sculpture in heroic proportion.

Once the sculptor had solved the technical and aesthetic requirements of transparent sculpture his vision necessitated new forms and materials. Six major sculpture commissions which now came his way including pieces for the campus of Stanford University, for the city of Anchorage, for the airports of San Francisco and Miami and for the Djerassi Foundation in Woodside, California, he turned to working in stainless steel. He now made monumental sculptures, welded together from large hexagonal facets of highly burnished stainless steel. These finely crafted sculptures are supported by thin points from which they rise to considerable heights. In these open structures voids alternate with the solid polyhedrons. The viewer walking through and around them is able to perceive constantly changing spatial patterns. Like Calder's stabiles, these sculptures seem to imply architectural environments. But the high polish on Beasley's surfaces provides additionally the reflection of sky and landscape and creates a total experience.

The work in bronze, which is the theme of this exhibition and which is indeed, central to his oeuvre, had its origin in 1987 when he was invited to the International Sculpture Symposium in Krefeld. He sent a cardboard model of his *Intersections* (1987) which was then meticulously enlarged into a sculpture of Corten steel five times its original size, retaining all the smooth surfaces and sharp edges of the original. Always very much interested in crystallography, Beasley christened the finished piece *"Titiopoli's Arch"* in homage to the early student of this science in Greece. The magnification showed him the possibilities of moving into a new direction in his work and in 1988 he began his bronze castings. Once again he found a way to fuse art and technology. In his sculptures of the last five years he has used the computer as his drawing board. Using a highly sophisticated computer enables him to visualize a constant change of forms almost instantly. Earlier, when working in Lucite, he was interested in capturing several views at once by means of transparency. Now the computer gives him the possibility to actually compose the work from all sides almost simultaneously as new cubes or angles are generated by pressing a few keys. Even in his earlier works, when he made assemblages of discarded objects, Beasley was not greatly concerned with a hand-made appearance of his sculptures. Like Conceptual artists, and perhaps like many fine artists throughout history, he places greater value on the intellectual than on manual skill. But now, instead of searching through industrial scrap for his components, he is able to generate them on the computer.

Using an advanced Hewlett Packard workstation, which was donated to him by the manufacturer to allow his experimentation, Beasley plays with different shapes, adds, subtracts, tilts and moves shapes around with great rapidity, creating interesting interactions of forms. He can achieve interpenetrations by moving shapes inside others.

He may do this for a period of days until he is fully satisfied with the emergent form on the printout. This is then transformed, again by computer, into planar, two-dimensional patterns. The artist next makes a book, indicating numbered sections which are now projected into three dimensions and seen from different angles. This serves as the guide for the construction of a cardboard verification model. At this point it is possible to go back to the computer to make alterations. Finally, the patterns are plotted onto a "foam core" panel made of polyester and paper. The foundry in Berkeley then burns out the foam core and pours bronze into the resulting cavities and the sculptural form is complete and ready for the addition of acids to create patinas which are an integral part of the piece. The patinas may be light or dark, warm golden orange, or cold blue-green and often graphic elements which the artist had scratched on the foam core will add additional surface texture.

The works thus produced remain totally authentic Beasley pieces. Their rich vocabulary includes cubes, disks, shafts, spheres, trapezoidal and columnar shapes and fascinating interfacings between these geometrical elements. Among the important inspirations for his pieces are early memories of the great buttes in Monument Valley in Arizona, a unique landscape which is truly breathtaking in its vast scale and incredible rock formations. These recollections are reflected in works such as *Mesa* (1992) and *Refuge* (1993). Beasley also speaks about the building blocks of natural forms as the source for his work, of crystals, bones and of molecular structure itself. It is worth noting that he has a large collection of many species of animal skulls in his studio.

Intersection which was the original work in this series consists of a tumble of cubes and a large strut extending the piece into space. Similar levitation occurs in *Bateleur* (1989), but now a shape, recalling an inverted obelisk juts down rapidly, creating an intriguing balance and suggesting the volume of a virtual circle, while in *Apparition* of the same year again a large number of various cubes accumulate at the end of a thrusting arm. Variations on this theme occur in *Thrust* (1991) and *Breakout* (1991). Then there are works such as *Precursor* (1992) in which cubical forms are piled up in masses that want to hug the ground on which they rest, while the somewhat similar *Uplift II* (1992) evokes a sense of rising as

suggested by the title the sculptor gave to this piece. Whereas his earlier work carried titles from Greek mythology, the more recent pieces are entitled with names that suggest their movement or their presence, such as *Ceremony* (1989) with its carefully broken columnar structure or *Spokesman* (1993) in which a very weighty top is supported by a relatively small shaft, creating a sense of astonishment in the viewer who wonders how the artist was able to achieve this precarious balance. *Pillars of Cypress* (1990), a rectangular shaft with blocks falling away from it, was named for the disaster during the Loma Prieta Earthquake of 1989, when a section of the Cypress Freeway was destroyed. There close to the place where Beasley had lived and worked for over thirty years, a number of people were killed and Beasley and his son assisted in the rescue efforts. Referring to the strength of his neighbors who came to the aid of the victims and to the failure of the freeway structure, he explains "It symbolizes the pillars of the neighborhood that stood when the pillars of the freeway failed."[7] This square column was followed by a number of related structures such as *Sentinel* (1990), *Tower of Silence* (1991) and *Watchtower* (1992), which is probably the most elegant work of this series. Two extended vertical shafts are connected by a horizontal bar at the top in *Ascender II* (1991). This work is 64" high but it could be envisaged on a monumental scale when it would serve as a noble ceremonial gateway. The artist has, in fact, designed a number of pieces on a scale too large to be cast. These works are fabricated in his studio and consist of sizable bronze sheets which are cut and welded together with invisible seams. The sharp edges and the minute accuracy of the fabrication is an essential part of an exacting aesthetic.

Beasley's recent bronzes, as his earlier work again manifest a synergism of art and science. These polyhedrons are crafted with the crisp precision of the industrial age: they were generated with the aid of post-industrial computers. But in the final analysis they are the product of the artist's vision.

Playing intellectual games like Herman Hesse's Magister Ludi, Bruce Beasley has recently begun to make drawings on the computer in which tilted perspectives and overlapping planes create unexpected shadows which makes us recall the mordant and mysterious shadows of De Chirico's metaphysical paintings. Like the sculptures he has made over a period of more than thirty years these drawings are able to stimulate both our minds and our emotions.

Peter Selz
Berkeley, Summer 1993

Notes

1. Herschel B. Chipp, "Introduction", *Onze Sculpteurs Americaine,* Berkeley, University Art Gallery, 1964. n.p.
   In addition to Beasley a number of other sculptors in this group were to attain recognition for important work. Among them were James Melchert, Charles Ross and Stephen de Staebler.

2. Andre Malraux, quoted in "A French Honor", *San Francisco Chronicle,* Feb. 4, 1964.

3. Henry Seldis, "Young Sculptor Displays Rare, Precocious Talent", *Los Angeles Times,* June 3, 1963.

4. Gabo and Pevsner, "The Realist Manifesto", in Herschel B. Chipp, Peter Selz and Joshua C. Taylor, *Theories of Modern Art,* Berkeley, The University of California Press, 1968, p. 329.

5. L. Moholy-Nagy, *Vison in Motion,* Chicago, Paul Theobald, 1947, p. 235.

6. Bruce Beasley in Michael Rogers, "The Sculpture Transparent", *Science,* vol.4, no 10 (December 1983), p.45.

7. Beasley in Janet Kornblum, "Out of the Rubble", *The Times-Star,* Oakland, May 2, 1990.

Ein Interview mit Bruce Beasley

MD: Sie haben sich selbst als Vertreter der Klassischen Moderne bezeichnet. Was kommt Ihnen dabei in den Sinn?

BB: Die traditionelle Definition der Moderne, die eine Verpflichtung beinhaltet an künstlerischen Ausdrucksweisen im Sinne von abstrakter Form und Gestalt - Ausdrucksweisen im Sinne des Nichtgegenständlichen und der gestalterischen - Veränderung von Ausgangsformen. Ich denke jedoch nicht, daß die Moderne ausschließlich das Abstrakte beinhaltet, auch wenn es ein wesentlicher Teil meiner Konzeption ist.

MD: Oft wird der Begriff der Moderne assoziiert mit Lehrmeinungen des Abstrakten, die nur die Form behandeln und den gefühlsmäßigen Ausdruck und das Narrative ausschließen. Ist dies die Meinung, der Sie sich auch anschließen?

BB: Ich fordere nicht den Ausschluß von Gefühlen, das wäre sehr kalt und steril. Tatsächlich glaube ich, daß das mit der Minimal Art geschehen ist. Ich bin dem emotionalen Ausdruck tief verpflichtet, aber am Narrativen bin ich nicht interessiert. Erzählung ist einfach nicht das Vokabular, das mich aussagen läßt, womit ich mich beschäftige, oder das Fragen zuläßt, die ich stellen möchte, oder das die Art ermöglicht, wie ich sie stellen möchte.

MD: Es gibt auch eine gegenständliche Kunst, die auf diese Art und Weise des Open-End funktioniert. Können Sie etwas spezifischer sein?

BB: Sagen wir, ich möchte Begriffe übermitteln wie Einsamkeit oder Fliegen oder Freiheit. Um Freiheit oder Fliegen auszudrücken, kann ich einen Vogel oder ein Flugzeug auf seinem anmutigen Flug am freien Himmel darstellen. Wenn ich das tue, habe ich für den Betrachter entschieden, was Fliegen und Freiheit bedeuten. Ich habe damit viele andere gefühlsmäßige und assoziative Möglichkeiten ausgeschlossen. So kann zum Beispiel ein Flugzeug für jemanden anderen nicht für Flug stehen, sondern für Krieg und Tod. Und was ist, wenn ich mich mit dem Flug der Gefühle beschäftigen will oder mit der Frage, was Fliegen eigentlich ist? Bei vielen Gefühlen und Fragen ist der Realismus einfach im Weg. Es ist viel interessanter und herausfordernder, zu versuchen, jemandem ein Gefühl zu entlocken, ohne ein erkennbares Objekt vorzustellen. Ich bin dadurch gezwungen, mein Gespür für das Wesentliche und das Innere einer Emotion zu schärfen, wenn es mir gelingen soll, Gefühl nur durch Form hervorzurufen.

MD: Es fällt auf, daß Sie das Fliegen als Beispiel nehmen, da viele Ihrer Arbeiten ein Gefühl der Schwerelosigkeit vermitteln.

BB: Ich glaube nicht, daß das Zufall ist. Konzepte wie Freiheit, Sichlosreißen, auf dem Grat zwischen Stille und Bewegung balancieren, sind profund und universell. Sie durchdringen fast jeden natürlichen Prozeß und lassen sich auf das persönliche Leben genauso wie auf soziale Strukturen anwenden. Viele Menschen spüren "Fliegen" in meiner Arbeit, aber man kann nie sagen, daß genau das ausgedrückt wurde. Es ist ein Vorschlag. Einige empfinden es so, andere nicht.

MD: Sagen Sie damit, daß Ihr eigener Standpunkt oder Ihre Botschaft keine Rolle spielen, daß Sie keine Stimme haben während Ihres Schaffens?

BB: Nein, das meine ich nicht. Die Arbeiten sollen kein Rorschach-Test sein, bei dem jede Reaktion ausschließlich aus der Erfahrung des Betrachters resultiert. Ausgangspunkt ist mein eigenes emotionales visuelles Vokabular. Durch dieses persönliche Vokabular sage ich Dinge, die für mich gültig sind und von denen ich hoffe, daß sie auch für andere stimmen. Was die Arbeiten sagen wollen, kann nur visuell ausgedrückt werden, eine Übersetzung der Arbeit ins Verbale ist nicht möglich. Da ich nicht schreiben kann, welche Erfahrung und Reaktion der Betrachter haben soll, fühle ich mich verantwortlich für die visuelle Welt, in die er eintreten soll, und ich konstruiere die emotionalen Wegweiser dorthin sehr sorgfältig. In diesem Zusammenhang denke ich an Musik, und darin stimme ich mit Kandinsky überein. Wir hören Musik, sie ist nicht direkt mit Worten oder Erklärungen oder einer Geschichte verbunden,

dennoch kann sie eine ganze Skala sehr grundlegender und doch gleichzeitig auch persönlicher Gefühle oder Wahrheiten hervorrufen. Das ist mein Ziel.

MD: Sie erwähnen sehr oft das Gefühl. Wenn ein nichtgegenständlicher Künstler das Gefühl betont, denke ich an die New York School. Würden Sie sich in eine Reihe stellen mit den amerikanischen abstrakten Expressionisten?

BB: Ich denke ja, aber ich würde den Begriff noch weiter zurückführen bis hin zu jener Tradition des abstrakten Expressionismus, der mit Kandinsky begann und weiterführte über Tatlin, Gonzalez und andere, bis er in den 40er und 50er Jahren auch hier Früchte trug. Ich denke, ich bin sehr eng mit der New York School verbunden, weil die Künstler mir zeitlich am nächsten sind und sicherlich auch wegen der Art, wie ich arbeite, nämlich das Werk sich schwerpunktmäßig aus dem Prozeß entwickeln zu lassen. Aber mehr noch als mit irgend einem anderen Künstler fühle ich mich mit Chillida verbunden. Die Klarheit seiner Formen, die Stärke der positiven wie auch der negativen Figuren, und die tiefe emotionale Reaktion, die sein Werk hervorruft, sind Qualitäten, die auch ich anstrebe.

MD: Im Blick auf die Bewegung Ihrer Skulpturen, die ja in Bronze nur schwer ausgedrückt werden kann, was meinen Sie, wenn Sie sagen: "das Werk sich aus dem Prozeß entwickeln lassen"?

BB: Ich habe das Gefühl, daß der Prozeß ein eigenes Leben hat. Ich entdecke das Stück, während ich es erschaffe, ich finde es eher, während ich daran arbeite, als wenn ich eine vorformulierte Vorstellung im Kopf hätte. Darin fühle ich mich der Spontaneität des abstrakten Expressionismus nahe. Wenn ich fordere, "das Werk sich aus dem Prozeß entwickeln zu lassen", dann spreche ich nicht von dem technischen Prozeß des Gießens oder Schweißens der Bronze, sondern ich spreche vom bildnerischen Prozeß des Arrangierens und Handhabens der Formen und des Raums.

MD: Sie sagten, der Raum sei für Sie ein lebendiges und faßbares Ganzes; was bedeutet das für Ihr Werk?

BB: Im Grunde genommen soll meine Arbeit das

Gefühl erzeugen, daß Raum ein faßbares Ganzes ist. Massen und Volumen durchschneiden ihn, bewegen sich in ihm oder kommen in ihm zur Ruhe. Ich sehe Raum nicht als leblosen Ort, sondern als ein lebendiges Ganzes, das tatsächlich auf die auf ihn einwirkenden Kräfte in Form von Gestalt reagiert. Ich sehe Gestalt und Raum sich gegenseitig halten, sich ausweichen, sich aufeinander pressen. Diese Vorstellungen beinhalten eine ganze Reihe expressiver und emotionaler Möglichkeiten. Wenn an einer Skulptur ein Teil einfach nur in den Raum ragt, erzeugt dies nur eine Erfahrung beim Betrachter. Ein ganz anderer emotionaler und kinästhetischer Effekt entsteht, wenn das gleiche ragende Teil das Gefühl vermittelt, daß es in den umgebenden Raum eindringt, ihn umschließt oder zusammenzieht. Dieses Gefühl kann nur erzeugt werden, wenn ich Raum als dynamisches Ganzes sehe und nicht als leeren Ort, und wenn ich mich wirklich frage, was Volumen, Masse und Schwerkraft sowohl logisch als auch emotional tatsächlich bedeuten.

MD: Sie haben betont, daß das formale Anliegen Ihrer Arbeit die Auseinandersetzung mit der Trennung von Masse, Volumen und Schwerkraft sei. Das ist ja naturwissenschaftlicher Fachjargon. Was genau bedeutet es in Bezug auf Ihre schöpferischen Ziele?

BB: Lassen Sie mich zuerst klarstellen, daß ich als Künstler nicht formale von inhaltlichen Anliegen trenne. Ich glaube nicht, daß man sie überhaupt trennen kann; Kunst ist die gut austarierte Form, die zugleich eine tiefgreifende emotionale Antwort formuliert. Hinsichtlich der Idee, Masse, Volumen und Schwerkraft zu untersuchen, sind meine Absichten mehr an meinen inneren als an naturwissenschaftlichen Anliegen orientiert.

Alles was wir durch die Naturwissenschaften oder durch unsere ureigensten Erfahrungen über die Welt lernen, vermittelt uns, daß Masse, Volumen und Schwerkraft interdependent sind; wir definieren das eine durch das andere. Wenn etwas viel Gewicht oder Masse hat, empfinden wir in unserem Inneren, daß das Volumen oder der Raum, der davon beansprucht wird, sich irgendwie proportional zum Gewicht verhält. Einfach ausgedrückt: etwas Schweres ist groß und braucht viel Platz. Wie Sie schon bemerkt haben,

wirken in meinen Arbeiten riesige Volumina oft schwerelos und von der Luft getragen, da ich die gängige Assoziation zwischen Volumen und Gewicht unterbrochen habe. Nehmen wir an, ich habe einen langen Bronzearm, der in den Raum hineinragt und einen Teil dieses Raums für sich beansprucht. Sein Volumen ist der Bereich, den die Form ausfüllt. Es erscheint uns logisch zwingend, daß jedes geformte Volumen Masse hat. Jetzt kann ich diese lange Form sehr subtil im Verhältnis zu sich selbst und zu anderen Formen verändern, so daß sie den Eindruck erweckt, sich zusammenzuziehen oder Raum in sich aufzunehmen. Das gleiche Volumen wird jetzt gefühlsmäßig und kinästhetisch mit einer anderen Masse erlebt. Irgendwie habe ich Masse und Volumen getrennt und kann sowohl die emotionalen als auch die logischen Komponenten benutzen, um mit dem Betrachter zu kommunizieren.

Ich muß allerdings hinzufügen, daß diese Trennung von Volumen, Masse und Schwerkraft, die ich zu erreichen versuche, nicht konkrete Aussage der Arbeit ist, sondern ein Mittel auf dem Weg zum eigentlichen Erlebnis. Der Betrachter spricht nicht aus, daß er irgend etwas davon erfahren hat. Es ist meine Aufgabe, all dies so auszuarbeiten, daß der Betrachter es einfach spürt - frei, leicht, irgendwo in seinem Inneren.

MD: Es scheint, als hielten Sie die Vermittlung von Ausdruck durch Abstraktion für die beste Aussageform. Haben Sie sich dem Gegenständlichen als künstlerischem Vehikel ganz verschlossen?

BB: Als "Empfänger" ganz und gar nicht. Meine Wohnung ist voll mit gegenständlicher Kunst. Ich bin ein fanatischer Sammler von nicht-westlicher Kunst und die primäre Sprache dieser Werke ist figurativ. Ich schätze auch die Arbeiten vieler zeitgenössischer Künstlerkollegen, die sich gegenständlich formulieren, z.B.: Manuel Neri, Wayne Thiebaud und Stephen de Stabler. Diese Künstler wecken in mir die gleiche gefühlsmäßige Antwort, die ich auch mit meinen Werken anstrebe. Jedoch als "Sender" künstlerischer Information fühle ich mich wohler bei der Abstraktion. Visuell und manuell kommuniziere ich besser in Form und Raum - ich schaffe fließender in dieser Sprache.

MD: Sind Sie ein guter Zeichner? Kommt der leichte

Umgang mit der Abstraktion durch technische Grenzen, die Sie im Hinblick auf das Figürliche empfinden?

BB: Nein, ich habe die ganze Ausbildung der Kunsthochschule absolviert. Es hat nichts mit Fähigkeiten zu tun. Ich fühle mich einfach wohler und es entspricht mir mehr, mich weniger spezifisch und eher evozierend durch Form auszudrücken.

MD: In vielem, was über Sie und Ihr Werk geschrieben wurde, werden Sie in Verbindung gebracht mit Naturwissenschaften, Mathematik und Technologie. Wie steht es damit?

BB: Das ist ein altes Vorurteil. Es hat mich viel Mühe gekostet, es loszuwerden. Ich habe mit einigem Vergnügen gelesen, daß ich ursprünglich Ingenieur gewesen sein soll oder Mathematik studiert haben soll. Das ist alles nicht war. An der High School war ich zwar damit beschäftigt, Rennautos zu bauen und auch Schmuck herzustellen. Ich merkte aber bald, daß meine Vorliebe für heiße Öfen mehr mit Ästhetik zu tun hatte als mit Mechanik, und daß man beim Fertigen von Schmuck schnell an intellektuelle Grenzen stößt. Für mich stand aber fest, daß ich mit meinen Händen Dinge schaffen wollte, Resultate der soweit als möglich vorangetriebenen manuellen und intellektuellen Fähigkeiten sowie der Vorstellungskraft. Auf diese Verbindung war die Bildhauerei eine ganz klare Antwort, und ich ging direkt ans College, um Kunst zu studieren. Offiziell habe ich nie etwas anderes studiert als Kunst.

MD: Wie steht es damit, daß so viel Ihrer Arbeiten mit Hilfe des Computers entstehen? Sicher hat das dazu beigetragen, diesen Techno-Mythos um Ihre Absichten und Ihren Werdegang entstehen zu lassen.

BB: Ich möchte dies ein für alle mal klarstellen. Auch ohne Hilfe des Computers würden genau die gleichen Arbeiten entstehen, es wäre nur schrecklich arbeitsintensiv. Bevor ich entdeckte, wie der Computer helfen kann, baute ich mühsam Pappmodelle, an denen ich minutiös und sorgfältig Kanten- und Winkelverhältnisse variierte und zeitraubende Änderungen ausführte, bis ich in meinem Inneren spürte, daß jetzt nichts mehr geändert und nichts mehr zugefügt werden konnte, bis die Formen mir das

Richtige sagten. Dann wurden sie in Bronze gegossen. Ich liebte die *Bilder,* aber ich war unzufrieden mit der Langsamkeit des Prozesses. Ich wollte mit dem gleichen Vokabular arbeiten, aber spontaner. Als ich auf die Computertechnik stieß, suchte ich nur nach Möglichkeiten, die Modelle schneller zu bauen, Möglichkeiten, die mir erlaubten, zwanzig bis dreißig winzige Änderungen an Kanten oder Winkeln in Minuten statt in Wochen auszuführen. Ich probiere Möglichkeiten aus und verwerfe sie auf einem sehr hoch entwickelten Computersystem, auf dem ich dreidimensional modellieren kann, und ich spiele mit den Kombinationen, bis ich die richtige gefunden habe. Mein Ziel ist es, ein fertiges Stück zu schaffen, das die Aussage hat, die ich von ihm will. Der Computer vereinfacht nur die Vorstellung der Komposition, bevor ich richtiges Material zuschneide. Der Computer trifft keine Entscheidungen und hat keine Ideen; er ist ein Werkzeug wie ein Meißel, sonst nichts.

MD: Sie müssen doch zugeben, daß es wie ein Widerspruch erscheint, wenn Sie sich selbst in einer Tradition sehen, für die es beim bildnerischen Prozeß auf die Hände ankommt und Ihre Hände ziemlich weit entfernt sind von Ihrer Arbeit.

BB: Ich sehe da keinen Widerspruch. Ich formuliere die Figuren auf meinem Computer mit Stiften und Skalen, deren Bewegungsabläufe ich mit der Hand steuere. Ich tippe keine Zahlen ein. Es ist, wie wenn man eine dreidimensionale Zeichnung fertigt. Wenn ich mit der Form zufrieden bin, lasse ich den Computer maßstabgerechte Schablonen entwickeln, nach denen ich dann aus einer Schaummasse Formen fertige und zusammensetze. Ich experimentiere mit Modellen immer und immer wieder, bis ich zufrieden bin. Dann wird die Arbeit in Bronze gegossen. Im eigentlichen kreativen Prozeß ist wenig Unterschied, außer daß er spontaner ist und ich die nichtssagenden Alternativen in wenigen Tagen statt in Monaten aussondern kann.

MD: Wie steht es mit der Qualitätskontrolle bei einer Arbeit, die so schnell entwickelt werden kann?

BB: Ich glaube nicht, daß die Spontaneität in den frühen Stadien des Prozesses sich nachteilig auf das ästhetische Urteil auswirkt. Ich würde eher sagen, das Gegenteil ist der Fall. Je mehr ich mich auf den emotionalen Inhalt der Figuren statt auf die technischen

Hindernisse konzentrieren kann, umso besser sind die Stücke. Ich kann jedoch nicht einfach einen Knopf drücken und den Computer den Entwurf in Bronze gießen lassen. Ich experimentiere mit jeder Arbeit in Maquetteform so lange, bis ich davon überzeugt bin, daß sie jetzt fertig ist für den Bronzeguß. Ich bringe auch nie eine Arbeit in die Gießerei, wenn sie noch ganz neu ist. Ich lasse sie immer noch eine Zeitlang im Atelier, damit ich sie nicht nur im "Glanz der Neugeburt" sehe. Deshalb werden einige nie zum Gießen geschickt. Alles andere läuft wohl so ab wie bei den meisten Bildhauern. Zum Guß werden die Modelle von Hand mit Wachs überzogen. In dieses ritze und kratze ich ein, um ihm eine interessantere Oberflächenstruktur zu geben. Schließlich trage ich die Patina auf. Noch mehr Handarbeit gibt es an den größeren Arbeiten, die nicht gegossen werden können, sondern die aus mehreren Teilen zusammengesetzt werden müssen. Ich bestimme jede Nuance von Kante, Oberfläche, Struktur, Patina und Spiegelung. Ich bestimme während des Polierens, Schmirgelns und der Strukturierung der Oberfläche, welche Flächen hart sind und welche weich. Ich kerbe die Oberfläche der Bronze von Hand, ganz gleich, wie groß das Stück auch sein mag, um die Andeutungen von Tiefen und Höhen sorgfältig kontrollieren zu können. Das ist ein mühevoller Prozeß, den kein Computer ausführen kann. Nur wenige Neuentwürfe werden in Bronze realisiert, denn die Auswahl ist nicht weniger anspruchsvoll, wenn ich mit dem Computer modelliere, als wenn ich von Hand arbeite.

MD: Lassen Sie uns ein wenig zurückgehen, um einen Überblick zu bekommen. In den 60er und 70er Jahren, bevor Sie anfingen mit Bronze zu arbeiten, schufen Sie transparente Arbeiten aus Acryl, von denen einige sehr rund und organisch waren, ganz anders als diese eher geometrischen Arbeiten.

BB: Das ist ein guter Vorschlag, ich glaube nämlich, daß damals die Vorstellung von mir als Technik-Freak aufkam.

MD: Benutzten Sie damals auch schon einen Computer?

BB: Nein, aber ich war damals schon entschlossen, die Mittel zu beherrschen, die ich brauchte, um meine Arbeit zu machen, und mich allein auf das Wichtige zu

konzentrieren. Ich habe keine Angst davor, etwas zu erfinden, um damit an das Wesentliche in der Kunst zu kommen. Interessanterweise sind die frühen Arbeiten zwar deutlich anders, aber der Ausgangspunkt war vergleichbar. Ich beschloß, mit durchsichtigem Material zu arbeiten, denn wenn ich eine transparente Form zum Durchschauen mache, die keine Farbe hat und in gewisser Weise keine klar zu beschreibende Oberfläche, dann nehme ich damit wieder diesen Gedanken in Angriff, daß Masse, Schwerkraft und Volumen interdependent sind. Wenn man durch diese frühen transparenten Arbeiten durchschaute, mußte man feststellen, daß die Oberfläche unklar und diffus war. Das Stück spiegelte den es umgebenden Raum und sein Licht. Man sah durch das Werk hindurch, und dabei kam die Frage auf, wo die Masse begann und wo sie aufhörte, nicht auf eine logische, aber auf eine emotionale Weise.

MD: Aber wenn ich mich richtig erinnere, gab es bei diesen Arbeiten auch eine revolutionäre Technik.

BB: Ich bin jemand, der davon überzeugt ist, Probleme lösen und Werkzeuge gebrauchen zu müssen, um meine Kunst schaffen zu können. So einfach ist das. Ich habe mein Haus und mein Atelier gebaut, ich bin ein geborener Tüftler, jemand, der Dinge macht. Als ich also kein Glas verwenden konnte, um meine Ideen von Transparenz und Oberfläche zu realisieren, und als ich erfuhr, daß die klaren Kunststoffe, die zu der Zeit verfügbar waren, nicht in den Größen gegossen werden konnten, die ich brauchte, begann ich, zum Thema Polymere zu forschen und das Ergebnis war eine neue Methode, Acryl in sehr großem Maßstab zu gießen.

Die Entdeckung dieses neuen Gußverfahrens war nichts anderes als das Ergebnis aus der Absicht, transparente Skulpturen zu machen. Es war nur Mittel zum Zweck - genauso wie der Gebrauch des Computers zum Modellieren. Ich erfand ein Acrylgußverfahren, daß heute noch verwendet wird. Ich benutzte technische Erfahrung einfach, um zu meinem Ergebnis zu kommen, aber diese dumme Behauptung, daß ich ein "Techny" sei, blieb an mir hängen. Technik ist mein Werkzeug, nicht meine Botschaft.

MD: Es ist eine merkwürdige Erfahrung, in Ihrem Atelier zu sein mit diesem riesigen Industrie-Computer, der aussieht, als ob er auch bei der NASA stehen könnte, und mit den architektonischen Metallarbeiten; und wenn man sich umdreht, sieht man am gleichen Ort Regale voller Knochen, Fossilien, Kristallen, Fragmenten der natürlichen Welt, die mit so viel Sorgfalt und Sensibilität aufbewahrt werden. Sind Sie eine geteilte Seele - verführt von den Wohltaten der Technik, aber nach der Natur verlangend?

BB: Erstens ist Natur viel mehr als Bäume und Wiesen. Sie beinhaltet auch Vulkane, Erosionen und Platten-Tektonik. Ich sehne mich nicht nach der Natur, da mein positives Verhältnis zu ihr gewissermaßen selbstverständlich ist. Ich habe mein Wohn- und Arbeitsumfeld, das in einem Industriegebiet liegt, zu einem Stadtwald verwandelt. Ich bewahre all diese Fossilien und Knochen auf, weil ich von Grund auf interessiert bin an der Struktur von Materie und Form, vielleicht auch an der inneren Struktur von Gefühlen. Unter die Oberfläche zu schauen, um zu sehen, wie die Teile sichzum Ganzen fügen, das ist für mich ein Gebiet immerwährender Faszination. Wenn man eine fertige Bronzeplastik betrachtet, sieht man Formen aus Metall. Nimmt man aber die Oberflächenillusion weg, so gibt es eine komplexe und exakte Art und Weise, in der Form, Volumen, Gewicht, Spannung, Kante, Kraft, Winkel, Zug, Druck und Schwerkraft in einer absolut perfekten und geordneten Figuration zusam- menpassen, die als vollendet gilt. Es ist wie die kristalline Struktur - die Logik ist da und braucht nur entdeckt zu werden. Es ist die gleiche endgültige Konfiguration, die das Pfannengelenk zur perfekten Lösung für die Hüfte macht.

Es gibt eine enge Parallele zwischen Erfolg in der Natur und Erfolg in der Kunst. In beiden Fällen ist der Erfolg erreicht, wenn nichts hinzugefügt oder weggenommen werden kann. Dann weiß ich, daß ich ein gutes Kunstwerk habe, wenn von ihm das Gefühl ausgeht, daß alles genau da ist, wo es sein sollte. Die Natur erreicht diesen perfekten Punkt zwischen Wechsel und Ruhe, zwischen Form, die sich entwickelt, und Form, die vollendet ist. Der Natur gelingt dies am leichtesten und nur mit seltenen Fehlern. Ich benutze den Computer, meine Hände, meinen Schweiß, Mühe, meine Werkzeuge und einige Assistenten... und trotzdem werfe ich immer noch viele Fehler weg während des Entstehungsprozesses.

Die Natur bleibt der ideale Führer und die große Quelle, ohne sie gäbe es keine Wärme, keine Herzlichkeit, und ich bestehe darauf, daß meine Arbeit beides haben soll.

Marlena Donohue / Bruce Beasley
Oakland, Kalifornien, Oktober 1993

An Interview with Bruce Beasley

MD: You have called yourself a classical modernist. What comes to your mind when you say that?

BB: The traditional definition of modernism that implies a commitment to artistic expression in terms of abstract shape and form—expression in terms of non representation and the manipulation of basic shapes. I don't, however, think of modernism as implying abstraction exclusively, although it is an important part of my conception of it.

MD: Often the term modernism is associated with abstract schools that deal in form to the exclusion of expression and narrative. Is that the school with which you align yourself?

BB: I certainly don't align myself with the exclusion of expression, that would be very cold and sterile. In fact I feel that is what happened to minimal art. I am very deeply committed to expression but I am not interested in narration. Narration is simply not a vocabulary that lets me express the issues that I want to deal with or the questions that I want to ask or the manner in which I want to ask them.

MD: There is a representational art that functions in that open-ended way. Can you be more specific?

BB: Lets say that I want to convey concepts like solitude or flight or freedom. To express freedom or flight I can limn a bird or an airplane in graceful flight across an open sky. Once I have done that, I've decided for the viewer what flight and freedom mean. I have closed off many emotive and associative options. For example, for some, an airplane may not evoke flight at all, but war and death, and what if I want to deal with the flight of feelings or the question of what is flight? For many emotions and questions, realism simply gets in the way. It is much more interesting and challenging to try to elicit an emotion without representing any recognizable object. It forces me to hone my own sense of the essence and core of that feeling if I am to be able to extract an emotion out of shape alone.

MD: It's funny that you should mention flight since much of your work evokes a kind of weightlessness.

BB: I don't think that's an accident. Concepts like freedom, breaking loose, balancing on the brink between stillness and motion—these are profound and universal—they cycle through nearly every process in nature and have applications to personal lives and social structures. Lots of people sense flight in my work, but you can never quite say that's exactly what is conveyed. It's a suggestion. Some feel it others may not.

MD: Are you saying then, that your own view point or message plays no part, that you have no voice as you create?

BB: No, that is not what I mean. I do not intend them to be a Rorschach test where any reaction comes purely from the viewers own experience. The pieces have to begin from my own emotional visual vocabulary. From that personal vocabulary I say things that are true to me and that I hope will be true to others. What the pieces say can only be said visually, there is no verbal translation of the work possible. So while I cannot write what experience and reaction I want the viewer to have, I am responsible for the visual world they enter, and I am very carefully constructing the emotional guideposts along the way. I think of music in this regard, and here I agree with Kandinsky. We listen to music, it is not associated with words or descriptions or a story in any direct fashion, yet it can evoke a whole gamut of very profound and at once personal feelings or truths. That's what I'm after.

MD: You have mentioned feeling a lot. When a non representational artist stresses feeling, I think of the New York School. Would you align yourself with the American abstract expressionists?

BB: I think I would, but I'd take the term back further to the whole tradition of abstract expressionism that began with Kandinsky and carried on in various incarnations through Tatlin, Gonzales and others until it took seed here in the 40s and 50s. I imagine I am most closely aligned with the New York School because they are closest to me in time and because of the way I work—my emphasis on letting the work evolve out of the process. Perhaps more than any artist I align myself with Chillida. His purity of form, the strength of both the negative and positive shapes, and the deep emotional reaction his work engenders are qualities I too strive for.

MD: Your sculptures have a gestural quality but its harder to see that in the medium of bronze. What exactly do you mean when you refer to 'letting the work evolve out of the process?'

BB: I feel my process has a life of its own. I discover the piece as I create it—I find it as I work rather than having a preconceived notion in my head. In this I feel close to the spontaneity of abstract expressionism. When I speak of "evolving out of the process", I am not speaking about the process of casting or welding bronze. I am speaking about he process of arranging and manipulating the shapes and space.

MD: You have said that space for you is an alive and tangible entity, what's the significance of this in the work?

BB: Basically, I want my work to create the sense of space as a palpable entity through which masses and volumes cut, reside and move. I see space not as dead air but as an entity which actually responds to the forces being placed on it by shape. I see shape and space as holding each other, avoiding each other, pressing on each other. These evocations have a very rich array of expressive and emotional possibilities. If a sculptural protuberance simply extends in space, you produce one kind of experience in the viewer. There is a very different emotional and kinesthetic effect if that same huge extension conveys the sense that it invades or grabs or contracts the space around and in it. This feeling can only be created if I am seeing space as a dynamic entity and not empty air, and if I am really asking myself what volume, mass and gravity really mean both logically and emotionally.

MD: You've stressed that your work is formally concerned with separating mass, volume and gravity. That sounds like pretty scientific lingo. What exactly does that mean in terms of your creative goals?

BB: First let me clarify that as an artist I do not separate formal and expressive concerns. I don't think you can ever separate them; that's what art is—well gauged form that generates a deeply felt response. In terms of this idea of looking at mass, volume, and gravity—my intentions are more visceral than scientific. Everything we are told by science as well as our gut experience of the world tells us that volume, mass and gravity are interdependent; we define one in terms of the other. If something has lots of weight or mass, we feel in our bones that the volume or space taken up it is somehow proportional to the weight. Put simply, something heavy is big and takes up a lot of room. As you noted, in my work often enormous volumes feel weightless and airborne because I have broken down the automatic association between volume and weight. Let's say I have a long bronze arm coming off a piece and extending into space to take up an area of that space. The area which that shape takes up is its volume and we think of this quality as somehow inviolable and logical—each bit of shaped volume has a mass. Then I come along and I manipulate that long extension very subtly in relation to itself and other shapes, so that it conveys a quality of contraction, or of gathering space into itself. The same volume is now emotionally and kinesthetically associated with a different mass. Somehow I have separated mass and volume and am able to use their emotional components as well as logical ones to communicate with my viewer. I need to add though that this separation of volume, mass and gravity that I try to achieve is not the subject of the work, it is really a means to an expressive end. The viewer doesn't articulate having experienced any of this, it's my job to work all this out so that the viewer simply feels it—freely, easily, somewhere in the gut.

MD: It sounds as if you feel that expression is best served by abstraction. Are you closed off to representation as an artistic vehicle?

BB: In the position of the receiver of the art, absolutely not. My home is filled with representational art. I am an avid collector of non Western art and the main language of that sort of work is figurative. I love the work of many contemporary representational artists, for example: Manuel Neri, Wayne Thiebaud, and Stephen de Stabler. These artists elicit in me the same emotive response I strive to create in my own work. However, as a sender of artistic information, I'm more comfortable with abstraction. I communicate better visually and manually in shape and space—

I create more fluidly in that language.

MD: Are you a good draftsman? Does this ease with abstraction come with technical limits you might feel with respect to the figure?

BB: No, I had all the standard art school training. It has nothing to do with ability. I simply feel more authentic and at home speaking less specifically and more evocatively through shape.

MD: In much of the writing about you and your work, you are linked to science, math and technology. What about that?

BB: That is an old association that I have had a hard time shaking. I've read with some humor reports that I was originally an engineer or a math major in college. That is very far from the truth. In high school I was involved with building race cars and making jewelry. I soon realized that my love of hot rods had more to do with esthetics than mechanics, and that making jewelry was intellectually limited. I did know, however, that I wanted to spend my life making things with my hands that were the results of pushing my imagination, hands and intellect as far as all three of them would go. Sculpture was the clear answer to this combination of interests, and I went directly to college to study art. I have never formally studied anything but art.

MD: What about the fact that so much of your work is computer assisted? I am sure that has helped create this techno myth about your intentions and process.

BB: I really want to get this straight once and for all. I would be making exactly the same kind of work without the aid of the computer, it would just be terribly tedious. Before I discovered how the computer might help, I would laboriously build cardboard models varying minute, subtle edge and angle relationships, and making time consuming alterations until that moment in the life of a piece when I had a feeling in my gut that nothing could be changed or added and the shapes said something true to me. I would then cast them in bronze. I loved the imagery, but I was dissatisfied with the slowness of the process. I wanted to work with the same vocabulary of shapes but more spontaneously. I was searching for a way to build the models more quickly when I came upon computer technology that allowed me to try out twenty to thirty miniscule alterations of edge or angle in minutes instead of weeks. I test and eliminate possibilities on a very advanced computer system that permits complex three-dimensional modeling and I play with the right combinations until I have what I am after. My goal is to create a finished piece that says what I want it to. The computer simply facilities my visualization of the composition before I cut any real material. The computer makes no decisions and has no ideas; it's a tool, like a chisel, nothing more.

MD: You must admit that there is a slight contradiction in placing yourself within a tradition that hinges on gesture and hands on process when your work is somewhat removed from your hand.

BB: I do not see a contradiction. I manipulate the forms on my computer interactively with hand controlled stylus and dials. I don't type in numbers, It is really quite a hands on process.. What it really feels like is doing a drawing in three-dimensional space. Once I am happy with the model, I then have the computer generate templates to scale and I make those out of foamcore and assemble them. I experiment with works in maquette form over and over until I am satisfied. It then goes to bronze. There is little difference in the actual creative process, except that it is more spontaneous, and I can more quickly eliminate the non evocative options in days rather than months.

MD: What about quality control in work that can be generated so quickly?

BB: I don't think the spontaneity of the early stages of the process is any detriment to esthetic judgement. My feeling is that the contrary is more likely to be true. The more my concentration is focused on the emotional content of the forms rather than technical roadblocks, the better the pieces are. However I cannot just push a button and have the computer produce the piece in bronze. I experiment with each piece in maquette form over and over until I am satisfied that it is ready to go on to bronze. I also never send a piece out to be cast just when it is newly made. I always let them sit around the studio for a while so that I am not seeing them in the "glow of new birth". As a result

some never go on to be made in bronze. The rest of my steps are much as any sculptor's. For the cast pieces, I hand apply a wax surface to each model, that is scraped and engraved to give a more interesting texture to the casting, and I apply the patinas. For the larger pieces that are fabricated in bronze rather than cast, there is a great deal of hands on work, I determine in a very hands-on way every nuance of edge, of surface, texture, of patina and reflectivity. I determine in the grinding, sanding and texturing stages just which planes will be sharp, which will be soft. I score the surface of the bronze by hand no matter how huge the piece so that I can carefully control suggestions of depth and light. It's a laborious process no computer could execute and I produce relatively few actual works because my selectivity is no less exacting if I am modeling with the computer or building manually.

MD: Let's go back a bit for perspective. Before these bronze works, in the 60s and 70s you made acrylic, clear pieces some of which were very round and organic and quite different from these more geometric works?

BB: That's a good point because I think that is when this idea of me as a technology freak began.

MD: Did you use the computer then as well?

BB: No, but I was equally determined to master whatever means I needed to produce the work and address the issues I felt were important. I'm not afraid to invent in order to get at the meat of the art. Interestingly enough, those pieces were overtly different, but the issues were similar. I decided to work in clear materials because if I am shaping transparent, see-through foam that has no color and in a sense no clearly delineated ending surface, I am once again challenging this notion that mass, gravity and volume are interdependent. When you looked through those early clear works, you had to acknowledge that surface was ambiguous and diffuse. As the piece reflected its ambient space and ambient light, as you looked through the piece, questions of where its mass began and ended were raised not in logical but in emotional ways.

MD: But if I recall there was some revolutionary technology associated with those works as well.

BB: I am a person who believes in solving problems and using tools in order to create my art. It's that simple. I built my house and studio complex, I am a natural tinkerer, a maker of things. So when I could not use glass to execute my ideas about transparency and surface, and when I was told that the clear plastics available at the time could not be cast in the sizes I needed, I did some research into polymers and came up with a new process for casting acrylic in very large scale. Discovering the new casting process was nothing more than a result of wanting to make transparent sculpture, really it was just a means to an end - very much like my utilization of modeling with the computer. I invented an acrylic casting process that is still in use today. I was simply using technology to get at my issues but this silly notion of me as some "techy" stuck. Technology is my tool, it has nothing to do with my message.

MD: It's an odd experience to be in your studio with this enormous industrial computer that looks like it could be at NASA and your architectonic works in metal and then turn to see in the same space shelves full of bones, fossils, crystals, fragments from the natural world preserved with so much care and tenderness. Are you a divided soul—seduced by all the benefits of technology but longing for nature?

BB: First of all, nature is much more than trees and meadows. It is also volcanos, erosion, and plate tectonics. I don't long for nature because I keep my relationship with nature going. I have turned my studio and home complex into an urban forest even though it is in a heavy industrial part of the city. I keep all these fossils and bones because I am basically interested in the structure of matter and form, and maybe the inner structure of feeling as well. Looking below the surface to see how the parts add up to make the whole is an area of perpetual fascination for me. If you look at a finished bronze sculpture you see shapes in metal. But if you peel away the surface illusion, there is a complex and precise way that shapes, volume, weight, tension, edge, force, angle, pull, push and gravity all fit together in that absolutely perfect and ordered configuration that registers as correct. It's like crystalline structure—the logic is there for you to discover. It's the same ultimate configuration that makes a femur and ball joint the perfect solution for a hip. There is a close parallel between success in nature and success in art. In both cases success is achieved when nothing can be added or removed. That is when I know I have a good piece of art, when it emanates that feeling of everything being just where it should be. Nature arrives at this perfect point between change and stillness, between form that is evolving and form that is complete; nature does this most easily and with rare mistakes. I use the computer, my hands, my sweat, toil, my tools and a few assistants...and I still throw away a lot of mistakes in the process. Nature remains the ideal guide and the great resource; without it, there is no warmth, no heart and I insist that my work have both.

Marlena Donohue / Bruce Beasley
Oakland, California   October, 1993

Metall - Skulpturen / Metal Sculpture   1960 - 1968

UNTITLED

Eisenguß, 1960 (Cast Iron)

102 cm. (40" h.)

INDICTMENT

Bronzeguß, 1960 (Cast Bronze)

30 cm. (12" h.)

TREE HOUSE

Eisen, Geschweißt, 1960 (Welded Iron)

61 x 38 cm. (24" h. x 15" w.)

CHORUS

Eisen, Geschweißt, 1961 (Welded Iron)

36 x 62 cm. (14" w. x 24" h.)

Collection Museum of Modern Art, New York

DRUID

Eisen, Geschweißt, 1961 (Welded Iron)

86 cm. (34" h.)

LEMURES

Eisen, Geschweißt, 1961 (Welded Iron)

49 x 38 cm. (19" h. x 15" w.)

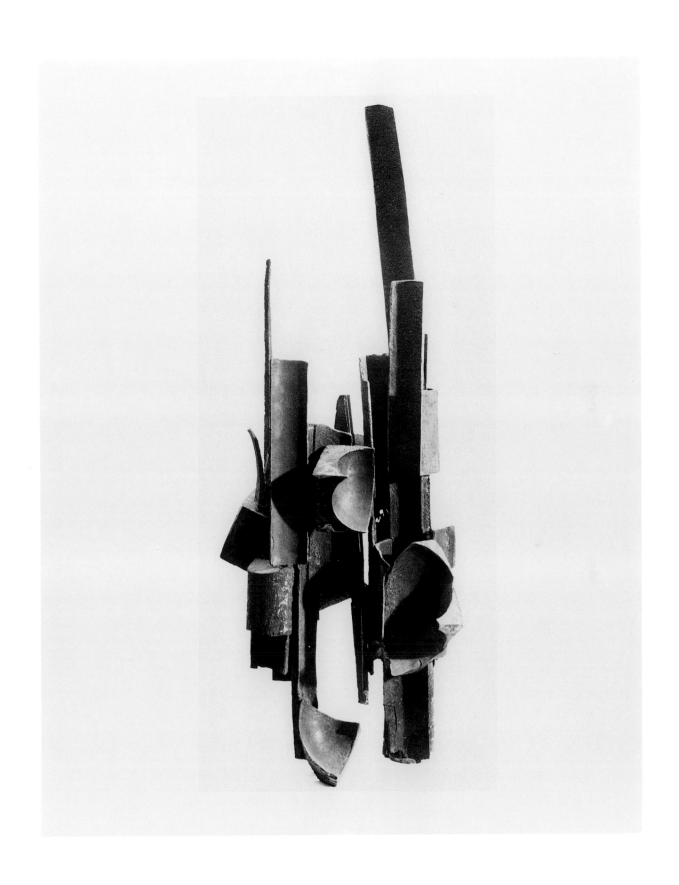

PROTEUS

Bronzeguß, 1961 (Cast Bronze)

92 cm. (36" h.)

PROMETHEUS

Aluminiumguß, 1962 (Cast Aluminum)

100 cm. (38" h.)

ICARUS

Aluminiumguß, 1963 (Cast Aluminum)

92 x 92 cm. (36" x 36")

Collection Musée d'Art Moderne, Paris

TYPHON

Aluminiumguß, 1962 (Cast Aluminum)

76 cm. (30" h.)

TALLOS

Aluminiumguß, 1962 (Cast Aluminum)

97 cm. (38" h.)

DARES

Aluminiumguß, 1962 (Cast Aluminum)

46 cm. (18" h.)

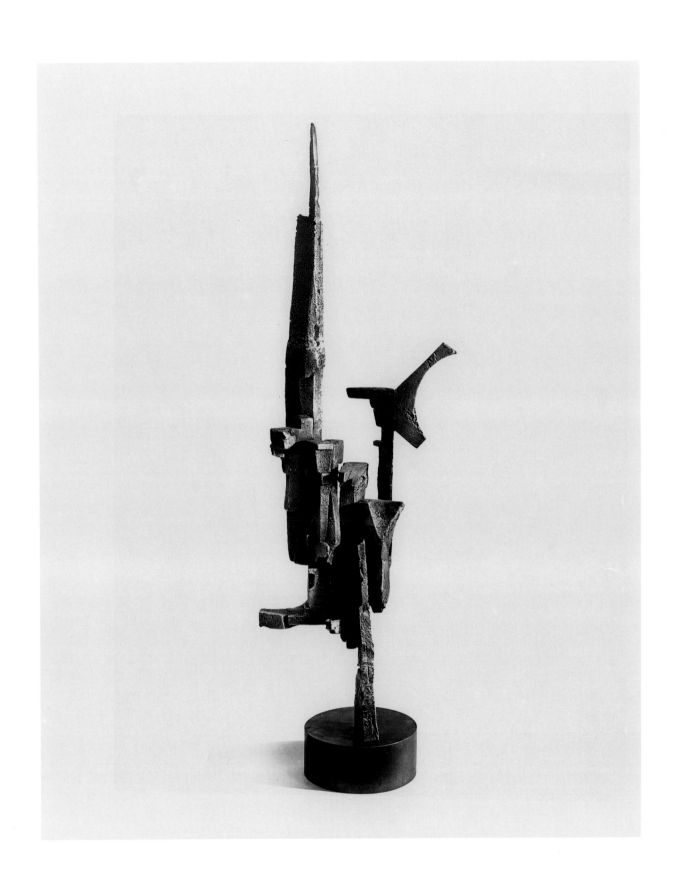

DARDANUS

Aluminiumguß, 1962 (Cast Aluminum)

107 cm. (42" h.)

ALKYONE

Aluminiumguß, 1963 (Cast Aluminum)

51 x 100 cm. (20" h. x 40" w.)

opposite

HEPHAISTOS

Aluminiumguß, 1963 (Cast Aluminum)

115 x 92 cm. (45" h. x 36" w.)

AMMON

Aluminiumguß, 1963 (Cast Aluminum)

66 x 46 cm. (26" h. x 18" w.)

DAEDALUS

Aluminiumguß, 1963 (Cast Aluminum)

97 cm. (38" h.)

Collection Los Angeles County Museum of Art

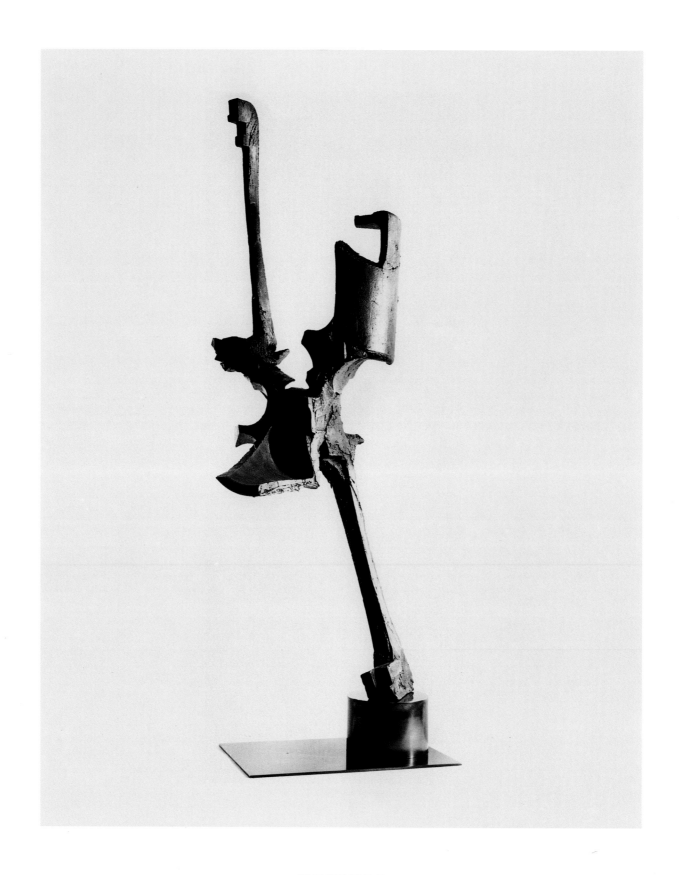

PROMETHEUS II

Aluminiumuß, 1963 (Cast Aluminum)

122 cm. (48" h.)

Collection Guggenheim Museum, New York

DIONE
Aluminiumguß, 1964 (Cast Aluminum)
100 x 104 cm. (39" h. x 41" w.)
Collection Franklin Murphy Sculpture Garden, UCLA

NIAD

Aluminiumguß, 1964 (Cast Aluminum)

130 cm. (51" h.)

DAMON

Aluminiumguß, 1964 (Cast Aluminum)

94 cm. (37" h.)

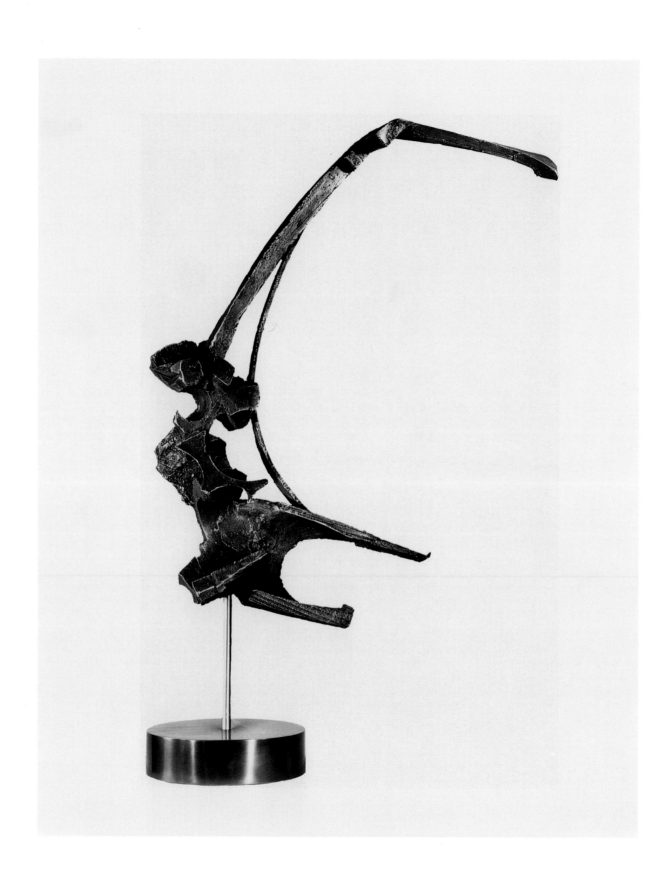

VASCONE

Aluminiumguß, 1965 (Cast Aluminum)
110 cm. (43" h.)

74

THESTOR

Aluminiumguß, 1965 (Cast Aluminum)

82 cm. (32" h.)

SMALL AMMON

Bronzeguß, 1965 (Cast Bronze)

36 cm. (14" h.)

CHIRON

Ahornholz, Montiert, 1981 (Maple Construction)
59 x 89 cm. (23" h. x 35" w.)

DANASTUS

Aluminiumguß, 1966 (Cast Aluminum)

102 x 46 cm. (40" h. x 18" w.)

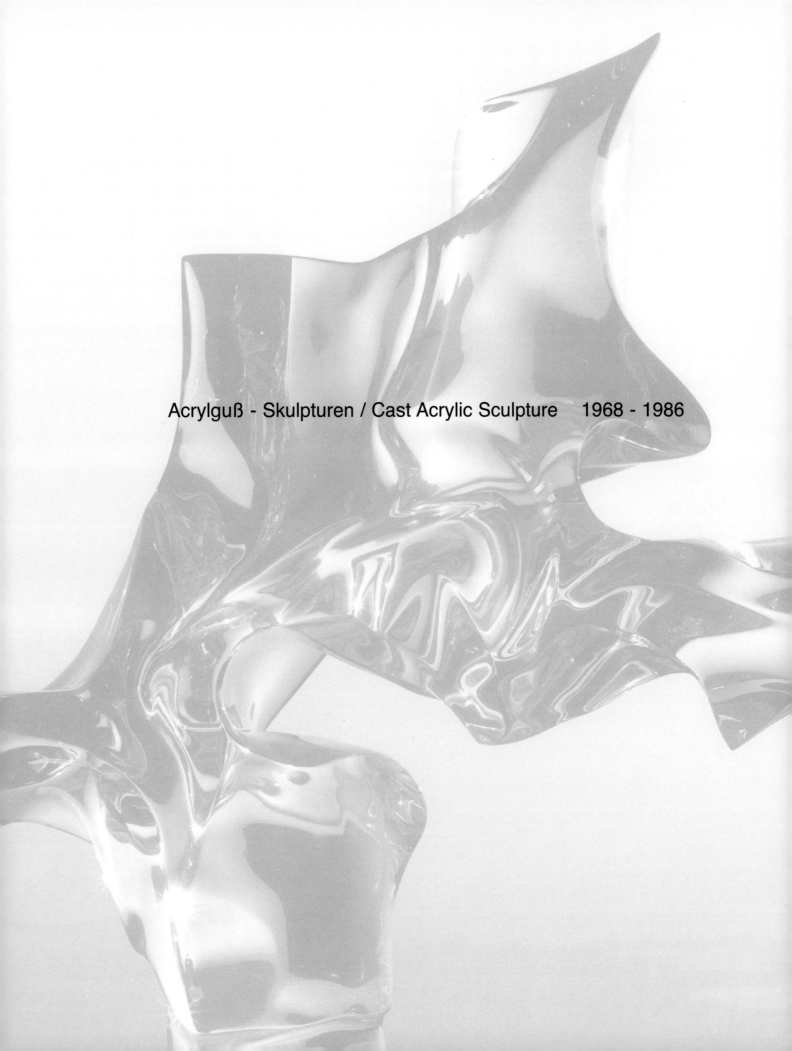

Acrylguß - Skulpturen / Cast Acrylic Sculpture   1968 - 1986

STAMPER'S LIGHTHOUSE

Acrylguß, 1967 (Cast Acrylic)

74 cm. (29" h.)

Collection The Crocker Art Museum, Sacramento, California

KLIKITAT

Acrylguß, 1968 (Cast Acrylic)

81 cm. (32" w.)

TIGIBUS

Acrylguß, 1968 (Cast Acrylic)

86 cm. (34" w.)

Collection Spencer Art Museum, University of Kansas

KILLYBOFFIN

Acrylguß, 1968 (Cast Acrylic)
112 cm. (44" w.)
Collection Harry W. Anderson

opposite

APOLYMON

Acrylguß, 1968-70 (Cast Acrylic)
275 x 460 cm. (9' h. x 15' w.)
Collection State of California, Sacramento, California

TRAPIDON

Acrylguß, 1970 (Cast Acrylic)

66 cm. (26" h.)

TRIGONAL

Acrylguß, 1970 (Cast Acrylic)

66 cm. (26" h.)

TRICLINIC ECLIPSE

Acrylguß, 1971 (Cast Acrylic)

94 cm. (37" h.)

TITIOPOLI'S LIGHT-HOUSE

Acrylguß, 1970 (Cast Acrylic)

87 cm. (34" h.)

Collection Hood Museum of Art, Darthmouth College

TRAGAMON

Acrylguß, 1972 (Cast Acrylic)
230 cm. (90" h.)
Collection The Oakland Museum

DODECKER

Acrylguß, 1970 (Cast Acrylic)

41 cm. (16" h.)

HEMIHEDRAL ECLIPSE

Acrylguß, 1971 (Cast Acrylic)

46 cm. (18" h.)

TECTODON

Acrylguß, 1972 (Cast Acrylic)

41 cm. (16" h.)

ATEADON

Acrylguß, 1972 (Cast Acrylic)
48 cm. (19" h.)

PECHEMELE

Acrylguß, 1972 (Cast Acrylic)

48 cm. (19" w.)

MONOCLINIC REPOSE

Acrylguß, 1972 (Cast Acrylic)

48 cm. (19" w.)

SCALAR GYRATION

Acrylguß, 1972 (Cast Acrylic)

61 cm. (24" w.)

Collection National Museum of American Art, Washington, D.C.

Acrylguß, 1978 (Cast Acrylic)
69 x 79 cm. (27" h. x 31" w.)

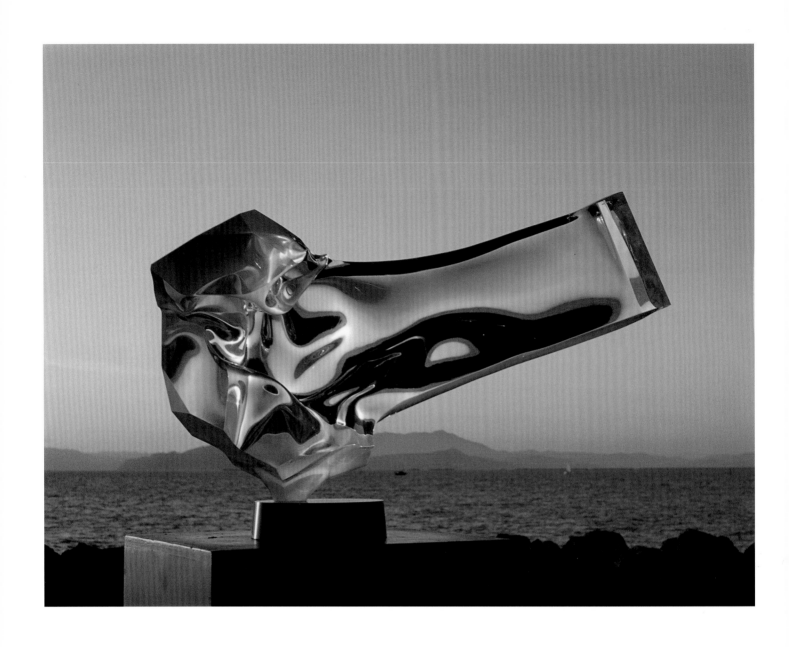

CIRCIS

Acrylguß, 1986 (Cast Acrylic)
53 x 100 cm. (21" h. x 39" w.)

Metall - und Holz - Skulpturen / Metal and Wood Sculpture   1980 - 1986

VANGUARD

Edelstahl, 1980 (Stainless Steel)

855 cm. (28' w.)

Collection Stanford University

THE HESPERIDES

Aluminium, 1980 (Aluminum)
670 x 1000 cm (22' h. x 32' w.)
Collection San Francisco International Airport

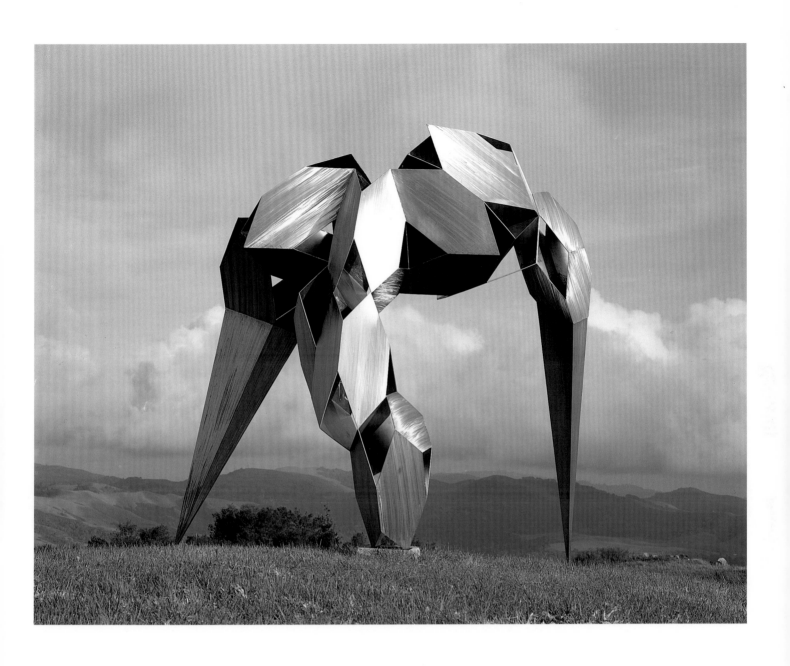

ARRISTUS

Edelstahl, 1981 (Staniless Steel)
430 cm. (14' h.)
Collection The Djerassi Foundation, Woodside, California

SMALL DORION

Ahornholz, Montiert, 1980 (Maple Construction)
100 x 150 cm. (39" h. x 59" w.)

ARTEUS

Ahornholz, Montiert, 1980 (Maple Construction)

79 x 155 cm. (31" h. x 61" w.)

THANA

Ahornholz, Montiert, 1981 (Maple Construction)

46 x 142 cm. (18" h. x 56" w.)

ARRISUS

Ahornholz, Montiert, 1981 (Maple Construction)
115 x 94 cm. (45" h. x 37" w.)

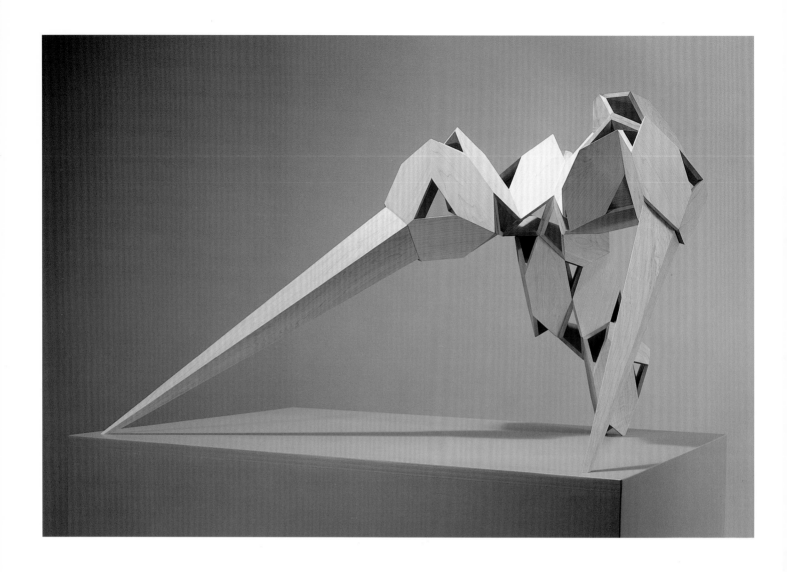

CHIRON

Ahornholz, Montiert, 1981 (Maple Construction)
59 x 89 cm. (23" h. x 35" w.)

opposite

TERINA

Bronzeguß, 1981 (Cast Bronze)
81 x 54 cm. (23" h. x 21" w.)

ARTEMON

Edelstahl, 1984 (Stainless Steel)

1000 cm. (32' w.)

ARCTOS

Edelstahl, 1985 (Stainless Steel)

1000 cm. (32' w.)

113

DORION

Edelstahl, 1986 (Stainless Steel)

920 x 615 cm. (20' h. x 30' w.)

Metall - Skulpturen / Metal Sculpture   1987 - 1994

TITIOPOLI'S ARCH

Cor-ten Stahl, 1987 (Cor-ten Steel)

300 x 340 cm. (9'8" h. x 11' w.)

INTERSECTIONS

Bronzeguß, 1987 (Cast Bronze)

61 x 84 cm. (24" h. x 33" w.)

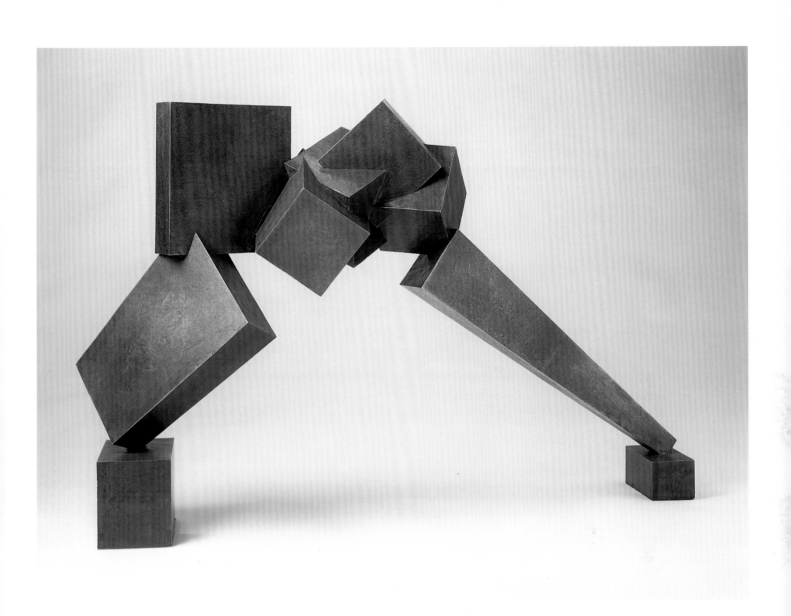

KEYSTONE

Bronzeguß, 1988 (Cast Bronze)

66 x 100 cm. (26" h. x 39" w.)

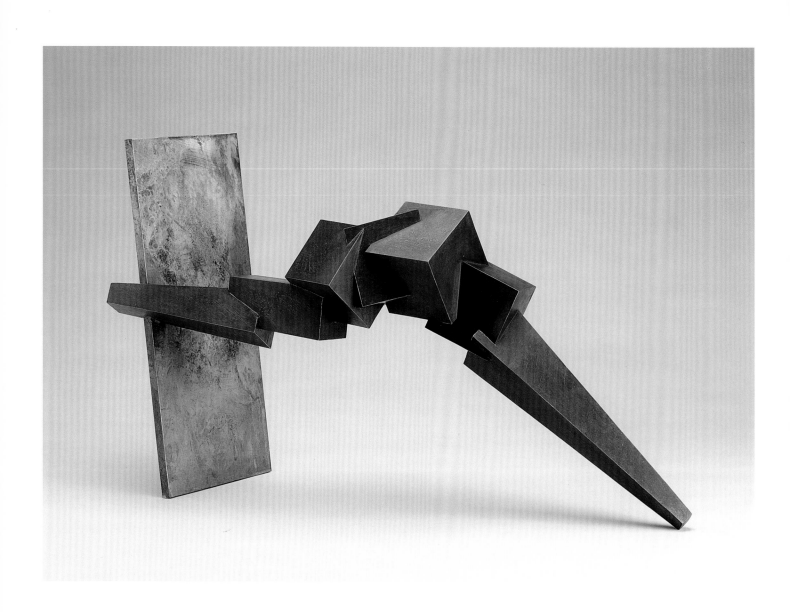

DEPARTURE

Bronzeguß, 1988 (Cast Bronze)

51 x 88 cm. (20" h. x 35" w.)

STORM

Bronzeguß, 1989 (Cast Bronze)

73 x 104 cm. (29" h. x 41" w.)

APPARITION

Bronzeguß, 1989 (Cast Bronze)

60 x 69 cm. (24" h. x 27" w.)

another view

APPARITION

Bronzeguß, 1989 (Cast Bronze)

60 x 69 cm. (24" h. x 27" w.)

BATELEUR

Bronzeguß, 1989 (Cast Bronze)

48 x 84 cm. (19" h. x 33" w.)

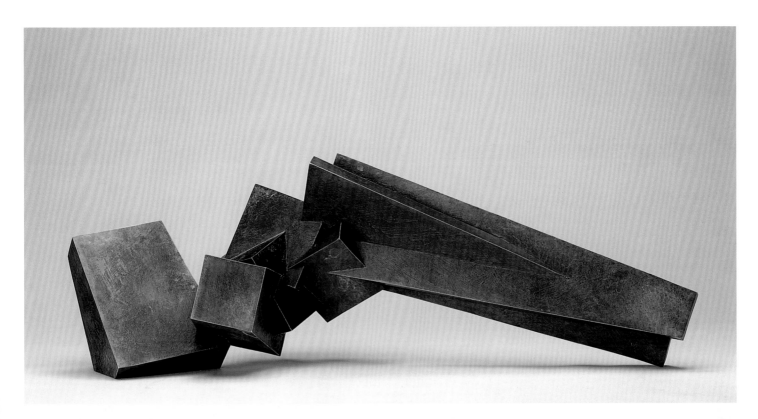

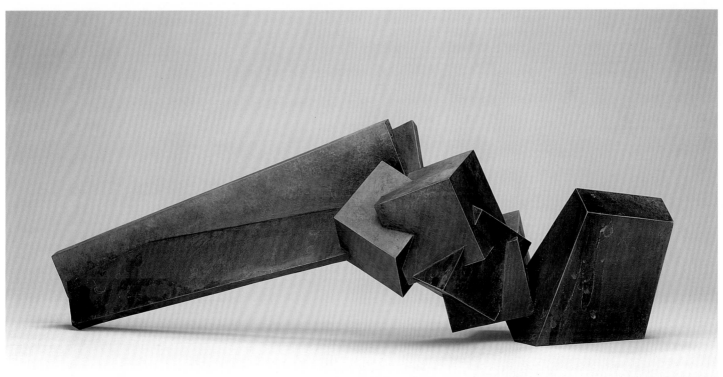

SEABORNE

Bronzeguß, 1989 (Cast Bronze)

35 x 105 cm. (14" h. x 41" w.)

CEREMONY

Bronzeguß, 1989 (Cast Bronze)

136 x 45 cm. (54" h. x 18" w.)

CERMONY

Bronzeguß, 1989 (Cast Bronze)

136 x 45 cm. (54" h. x 18" w.)

BATELEUR II

Bronzeguß, 1989 (Cast Bronze)

97 cm x 168 cm. (38" h. x 66" w.)

Collection Sheldon Memorial Art Gallery, Univeristy of Nebraska

SENTINEL

Bronzeguß, 1990 (Cast Bronze)

71 x 28 cm. (28" h. x 11")

PILLARS OF CYPRESS

Stahlguß, 1990 (Cast Steel)

135 x 43 cm. (53" h. x 17" w.)

TENACITY

Bronzeguß, 1990 (Cast Bronze)

54 x 45 cm. (22" h x 18" w.)

PILLARS OF CYPRESS II

Bronzeguß, 1990 (Cast Bronze)

88 x 28 cm. (35" h. x 11" w.)

TOWER OF SILENCE

Bronzeguß, 1991 (Cast Bronze)

61 x 28 cm. (24" h. x 11" w.)

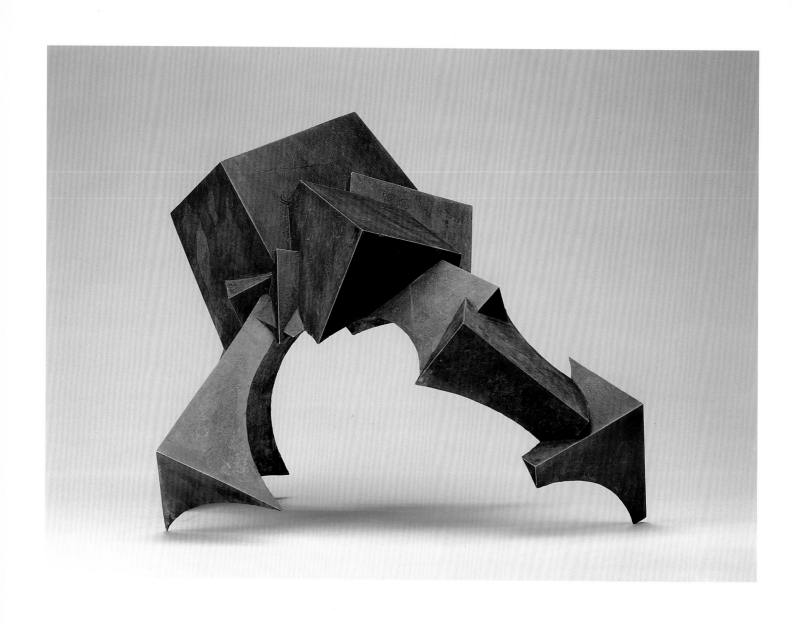

RAPTOR

Bronzeguß, 1990 (Cast Bronze)

48 x 61 cm. (19" h. x 24" w.)

another view

RAPTOR

Bronzeguß, 1990 (Cast Bronze)

48 x 61 cm. (19" h. x 24" w.)

INTERSECTIONS II

Bronzeguß, 1991 (Bronze)

262 x 350 cm. (102" h. x 140" w.)

opposite

ASCENDER

Bronzeguß, 1991 (Cast Bronze)

81 x 61 cm. (32" h. x 24" w.)

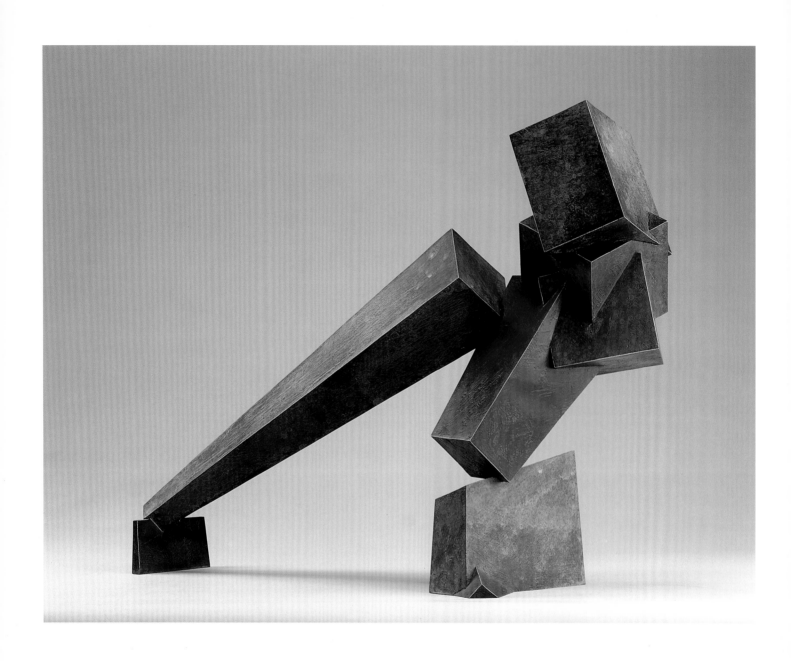

THRUST

Bronzeguß, 1991 (Cast Bronze)

63 x 80 cm. (25" h. x 32" w.)

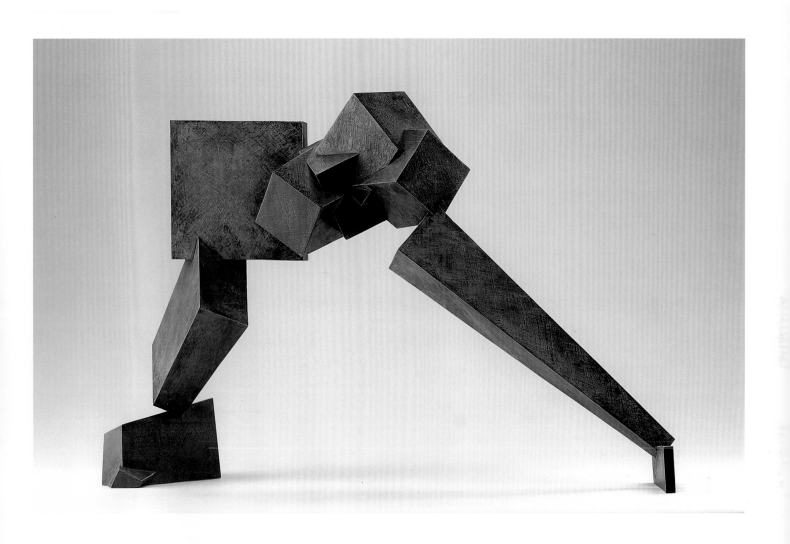

BREAKOUT

Bronzeguß, 1991 (Cast Bronze)

72 x 111 cm. (28" h. x 44" w.)

PRECURSOR

Bronzeguß, 1992 (Cast Bronze)

26 x 50 cm. (10" h. x 20" w.)

140

MESA

Bronzeguß, 1992 (Cast Bronze)

36 x 45 cm. (16" h. x 17" w.)

UPLIFT

Bronzeguß, 1992 (Cast Bronze)

17 x 45 cm. (7" h. x 18" w.)

opposite

KNIGHT'S GAMBIT

Bronzeguß, 1991 (Cast Bronze)

64 x 77 cm. (25" h. x 32" w.)

UPLIFT II

Bronze, 1992 (Bronze)

89 x 195 cm. (35" h. x 77" w.)

opposite

WATCHTOWER

Bronzeguß, 1992 (Cast Bronze)

96 x 38 cm. (38" h. x 15" w.)

another view

REFUGE

Bronzeguß, 1993 (Cast Bronze)

61 x 56 cm. (24" h. x 22" w.)

UPTHRUST

Bronzeguß, 1993 (Cast Bronze)

49 x 40 cm. (19" h. x 16" w.)

SPOKESMAN

Bronzeguß, 1993 (Cast Bronze)

91 x 18 cm. (36" h. x 7" w.)

MESSENGER

Bronzeguß, 1993 (Cast Bronze)

91 x 18 cm. (36" h. x 7" w.)

CONVERGENCE

Bronzeguß, 1993 (Cast Bronze)

51 x 68 cm. (20" h. x 27" w.)

opposite

FORAY

Bronzeguß, 1993 (Cast Bronze)

82 x 75 cm. (32" h. x 30" w.)

SOLID SEQUENCE

Bronzeguß, 1993 (Cast Bronze)

86 x 34 cm. (34" h. x 21" w.)

ASCENDER II

Bronzeguß, 1991 (Cast Bronze)

163 x 125 cm. (64" h. x 49" w.)

SENTINEL II

Bronze, 1991

204 x 71 cm. (80" h. x 28" w.)

MESSENGER II

Bronze, 1993

400 x 77 cm. (157" h. x 30" w.)

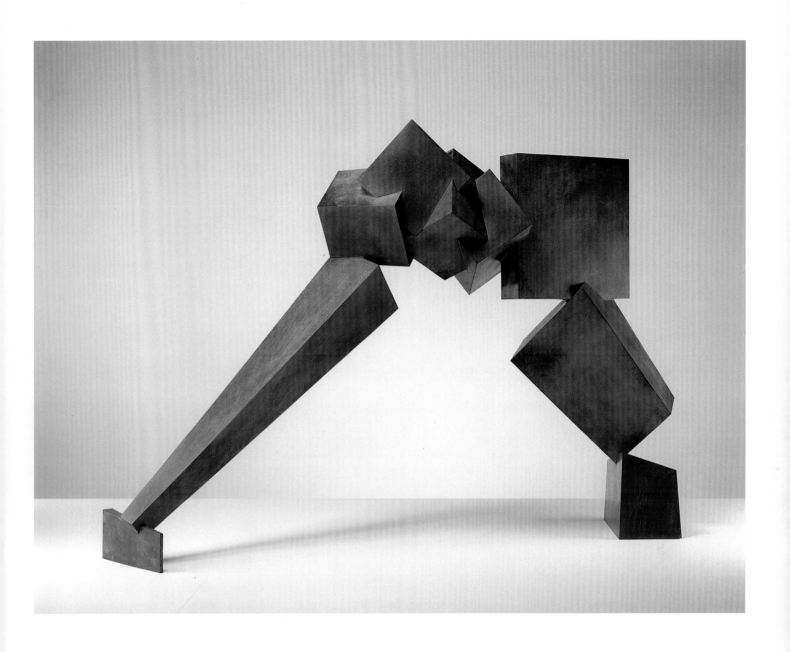

BREAKOUT II

Bronze, 1992

145 x 229 cm. (57" h. x 90" w.)

opposite

KNIGHT'S GAMBIT II

Bronzeguß, 1992 (Cast Bronze)

127 x 153 cm. (50" h. x 60" w.)

MESA II

Bronzeguß, 1993 (Cast Bronze)

137 x 170 cm. (54" h. x 67" w.)

WATCHTOWER II

Bronze, 1993

297 x 107 cm. (117" h. x 42" w.)

SPOKESMAN II

Bronze, 1994

366 x 74 cm. (144" h. x 29" w.)

BRUCE BEASLEY

BORN / GEBOREN   1939 in Los Angeles, California

EDUCATION / AUSBILDUNG   Dartmouth College, Hanover, New Hampshire, 1957-59
                                  University of California, Berkeley, California, B.A. 1962

MUSEUM COLLECTIONS / MUSEEN

Museum of Modern Art, New York
Solomon R. Guggenheim Museum, New York
Musée d'Art Moderne, Paris, France
National Museum of American Art, Washington, D.C.
Fine Arts Museums, San Francisco, California
Los Angeles County Art Museum, Los Angeles
Santa Barbara Museum of Art, Santa Barbara, California
The Oakland Museum, Oakland, California
San Jose Museum of Art, San Jose, California
Sheldon Memorial Art Gallery, University of Nebraska, Lincoln, Nebraska
Hood Museum of Art, Dartmouth College, Hanover, New Hampshire
University of Kansas, Spencer Museum of Art, Lawrence, Kansas
Franklin D. Murphy Sculpture Garden, University of California at Los Angeles
The Crocker Art Museum, Sacramento, California
Wichita Art Museum, Wichita, Kansas
Fresno Art Museum, Fresno, California
Xantus Janos Museum, Gyor, Hungary

SOLO EXHIBITIONS / EINZEL AUSSTELLUNGEN

1994	Städtische Kunsthalle Mannheim, Germany
1993	Galerie Scheffel, Bad Homburg, Germany
	Shidoni Gallery, Santa Fe, New Mexico
	Galerie Utermann, Dortmund, Germany
	Hooks-Epstein Gallery, Houston, Texas
1992	The Oakland Museum, Oakland, California
	Fresno Art Museum, Fresno, California
	California State University, Turlock, California
	John Natsoulas Gallery, Davis, California
	Jaffe Baker Gallery, Boca Raton, Florida
1991	California Polytechnic State University, San Luis Obispo, California
	Sonoma State University, Rohnert Park, California
	Southern Oregon State University, Ashland, Oregon
1990	Pepperdine University Art Gallery, Malibu, California
	Loma Linda University Art Gallery, Riverside, California
	Hooks-Epstein Gallery, Houston, Texas
1981	Fuller-Goldeen Gallery, San Francisco, California
1973	San Diego Museum of Art, San Diego, California
	Santa Barbara Museum of Art, Santa Barbara, California
1972	M.H. deYoung Memorial Museum, San Francisco, California
1971	Andre Emmerich Gallery, New York, New York

1966   David Stuart Gallery, Los Angeles, California
1965   Hansen Gallery, San Francisco, California
1964   Kornblee Gallery, New York, New York
1963   Everett Ellin Gallery, Los Angeles, California
1961   Richmond Art Center, Richmond, California

SELECTED GROUP EXHIBITIONS / GRUPPEN AUSSTELLUNGEN (AUSWAHL)

1994   *Sculpture Invitational*, Landesgartenschau, Fulda, Germany
        Art Frankfurt, Messe Frankfurt, Germany
        Contemporary Cast Iron Art, Visual Arts Gallery, University of Alabama at Birmingham
        Beasley, Dykes, Yates, Solomon Dubnick Gallery, Sacramento, California
1993   *International Biennial of Graphic Arts*, Xantus Janos Museum, Gyor, Hungary
        Art Frankfurt, Messe Frankfurt, Germany
        Chicago International Art Exposition, Donnelley International Hall, Illinois
        Fujisankei International Biennale: Excellent Maquettes, Hakone Open-Air Museum, Hakone, Japan
        Five Bay Area Sculptors, Harcourts Gallery, San Francisco, California
1992   *California Greats*, Syntex Corp. Gallery, Palo Alto, California
        New Works: Beasley, Albuquerque, Davis, Valerie Miller Fine Art, Palm Desert, California
        The 7th International Los Angeles Art Fair, Los Angeles, California
1991   *Sculptural Perspectives for the Nineties*, Muckenthaler Cultural Center, Fullerton, California
        Vernissage, Galerie Utermann, Dortmund, Germany
        New California Sculpture, The Oakland Museum, Oakland, California
1990   *Oakland's Artists '90,* The Oakland Museum, Oakland, California
1989   *Bay Area Bronze,* Civic Arts Gallery, Walnut Creek, California
1988   *State of California, Art in Public Buildings 1978-88,* Fresno State University, Traveled Statewide
1987   *Monumenta*, 19th Sculpture Biennale, Middleheim Sculpture Park, Antwerp, Belgium
        Steel Sculpture, International Steel Sculpture Symposium at *Park der Berg,* Krefeld, West Germany;
                Wantipark, Dordrecht, Netherlands; Yorkshire Sculpture Park, West Bretton, Great Britain;
                Kunsthalle Bremen, West Germany
        Budapest Triennial International Sculpture Exhibition, Palace of Exhibitions, Budapest, Hungary
        Sculpture - Modern and Contemporary, Anchorage Museum of History and Art, Anchorage; traveled to
                Alaska State Museum, Juneau, and University of Fairbanks
1986   *A Gift of Sculpture,* San Francisco Civic Center Plaza, sponsored by The San Francisco Arts Commission
        Casting Across America, North Dakota Museum of Art, Grand Forks, North Dakota
        Sculpture Invitational, Kaiser Center Roof Garden, Oakland
1985   *The Art of the San Francisco Bay Area: 1945 to 1980,* The Oakland Museum, Oakland, California
        Going Public: A Retrospective Exhibition, Walnut Creek Civic Arts Gallery and Civic Park,
                Walnut Creek, California
        Art Collectors In and Around Silicon Valley, Euphrat Gallery, DeAnza College, Cupertino, California
1984   *California Sculpture Show,* XXII Olympic Arts Festival and the Fisher Galleries, University of
                Southern California. Traveling exhibition to: Musee d'Art Contemporain de Bordeaux,
                France; Kunsthalle Mannheim, Germany; Yorkshire Sculpture Park, West Bretton, Great
                Britain; Sonja Henies Og Niels, Onstads, Norway, 1984-85
1983   *Outdoor Sculpture Show,* Shidoni Gallery, Tesuque, New Mexico
1982   *100 Years of California Sculpture,* The Oakland Museum, Oakland, California
        Northern California Art of the Sixties, deSaisset Museum, Santa Clara University, Santa Clara,
                California
        Forgotten Dimension, two-year tour organized by the Fresno Art Museum, Fresno, California
        The Shoebox Sculpture Show, University of Hawaii; traveled internationally, 1982-84
1980   *Forty American Sculptors,* XII International Sculpture Conference, Washington, D.C.
        Across the Nation, National Museum of American Art, Washington, D.C.
1979   *Acquisitions 1974-1978*, Dartmouth College Museum & Galleries, Hanover, New Hampshire
        Spaces, Walnut Creek Civic Arts Gallery, Walnut Creek, California

1976   *Fine Art in New Federal Buildings,* New Orleans Museum of Art, New Orleans, Louisiana
1975   *Public Sculpture-Urban Environment,* The Oakland Museum, Oakland, California
1974   *Oregon International Sculpture Symposium,* Eugene, Oregon
        Contemporary American Painting and Sculpture, Krannert Art Museum, University of Illinois,
            Urbana-Champaign, Illinois
1973   *Salon d'Mai,* The Luxembourg Gardens, Paris, France
        Salon de la Jeune Sculpture, Musee d'Art Moderne, Paris,France
        Refracted Images, DeCordova Museum, Worcester, Massachusetts
1972   *Sculpture '72,* Stanford University Museum of Art, Stanford, California
1971   *Translucent and Transparent Art,* Museum of Fine Arts, St. Petersburg, Florida
        Centennial Exhibition, San Francisco Art Institute, de Young Museum, San Francisco
        A Decade in the West, Stanford University Museum of Art, Stanford, California, and Santa Barbara
        Museum of Art, Santa Barbara, California
1970   *1970 Biennial Invitational,* Crocker Art Museum, Sacramento, California
        American Sculpture in Perspective, Sheldon Art Gallery, University of Nebraska, Lincoln, Nebraska
        Pierres de Fantaisie, The Oakland Museum, Oakland, California
        Excellence, University of California Art Museum, Berkeley
        Pollution Show, The Oakland Museum, Oakland, California
        Looking West, Josyln Art Museum, Omaha, Nebraska
        Sculpture Here and Now, Stanford University Art Museum, Stanford, California
        Expo '70, San Francisco Pavilion, Osaka, Japan
        A Plastic Presence, The Jewish Museum, New York; Milwaukee Art Center, Milwaukee, Wisconsin;
        San Francisco Museum of Modern Art, San Francisco, 1969-70
1969   *Plastics and New Art,* Institute of Contemporary Art, University of Pennsylvania,
            Philadelphia, Pennsylvania
        Contemporary American Painting and Sculpture, Krannert Art Museum,
            University of Illinois, Urbana-Champaign, Illinois
1968   *Art from California,* Janie C. Lee Gallery, Dallas, Texas
1967   *California Artists in National Collections,* Lytton Center of Visual Arts, Los Angeles, California
        Thirtieth Anniversary Exhibition, Richmond Art Center, Richmond, California
        Plastics West Coast, Hansen-Fuller Gallery, San Francisco, California
1966   *Selected Acquisitions,* Solomon R. Guggenheim Museum, New York
        Twenty-Two Sculptors, California State University at Northridge, California
        Annual Exhibition, San Francisco Museum of Modern Art, San Francisco, California
        Contemporary Art from the Lytton Collection, Lytton Center of the Visual Arts,
            Los Angeles, California,
1965   *Zellerbach Memorial Competition,* Palace of the Legion of Honor, San Francisco, California
        Some Aspects of California Painting and Sculpture, La Jolla Art Museum, La Jolla, California
        Annual Exhibition, San Francisco Museum of Modern Art, San Francisco, California
1964   *Contemporary Sculpture,* Albright Knox Gallery, Buffalo, New York
        Eleven American Sculptors, University of California Art Museum, Berkeley, California
        Group show, The Berkeley Gallery, Berkeley, California
1963   *Biennale de Paris,* Musee d'Art Moderne, Paris, France
        Contemporary California Sculpture, The Oakland Museum, Oakland, California
        Annual Exhibition, San Francisco Museum of Modern Art, San Francisco, California
        International Contemporary Sculpture, Everett Ellin Gallery, Los Angeles, California
1962   *Painting and Sculpture Acquisitions,* Museum of Modern Art, New York
        Three Artists, Gallery 8, Santa Barbara, California
1961   *Art of Assemblage,* Museum of Modern Art, New York; traveled to the Dallas Museum
            for Contemporary Art, and the San Francisco Museum of Modern Art, 1961-62
        Annual Exhibition, San Francisco Museum of Modern Art, San Francisco, California
        Contemporary Painting and Sculpture, Everett Ellin Gallery, Los Angeles, California
1960   *Northern California Sculptors Annual,* The Oakland Museum, Oakland, California
        Painting and Sculpture Annual, Richmond Art Center, Richmond, California

AWARDS AND PRIZES / AUSZEICHNUNGEN UND PREISE

1989   Individual Artist Award, Oakland Chamber of Commerce, Oakland, California
1967   Purchase Prize, San Francisco Arts Festival, San Francisco
1965   Frank Lloyd Wright Memorial Purchase Award, Marin Museum Association, San Rafael, California
1963   Andre Malraux Purchase Prize, Biennale de Paris, France
1961   Honorable Mention, San Francisco Museum of Modern Art Annual
1960   Adele Morrison Memorial Medal, The Oakland Museum Sculpture Annual

CIVIC AND CORPORATE COLLECTIONS / PRIVATE UND ÖFFENTLICHE SAMMLUNGEN

Arco Corporation, Los Angeles
Capitol Group, Los Angeles
City of Anchorage, Alaska
City of Eugene, Oregon
City of Salinas, California
Djerassi Foundation, Woodside, California
Federal Home Loan Bank, San Francisco, California
Federal Office Building, San Diego, California, GSA Art in Public Buildings
Gallaudet College, Washington, D.C.
Gateway Center, Walnut Creek, California
IBM Corporation, New York, New York
Kleinewefers GmbH, Krefeld, Germany
Lakeside Mall, Sterling Heights, Michigan
Mall at Short Hills, Short Hills, New Jersey
Miami International Airport, Miami, Florida
San Francisco Arts Commission, San Francisco, California
San Francisco International Airport, San Francisco, California
Security Pacific Corporation, Los Angeles, California
Stanford University, Stanford, California (2 pieces)
State of Alaska, Anchorage, Alaska
State of California, Capitol Office Building, Sacramento, California
State of California, State Office Building, San Bernardino, California
The Johnson Foundation, Racine, Wisconsin
Times Mirror Corporation, Los Angeles, California
Tupperware, Inc., Orlando, Florida
World Savings, Oakland, California

BOOKS / PUBLIKATIONEN

Maquet, Jacques. *The Aesthetic Experience.* Yale University Press, 1986.

Preble, Duane & Sara. *Artforms.* 5th Ed. Harper Collins Publishers, 1994.

Nawrocki, Dennis A., *Art in Detroit Public Places.* Wayne State University Press, 1980.

Seitz, William. *The Art of Assemblage.* The Museum of Modern Art, 1961.

Orr-Cahall,Christina., *The Art of California.* The Oakland Museum and Chronicle Books, 1984.

Albright, Thomas, *The Art of the San Francisco Bay Area: 1945 to 1980.* University of California Press, 1985.

Faulkner, Ray & Ziegfield, Edwin. *Art Today,* Holt Rinehart and Winston, 1969.

Krantz, Les, *The California Art Review.* American References Inc, 1989.

Osborne, Charles. *Nature-Science Annual: A Captive Flow of Light.* Time-Life Books, 1970.

Bush, Julia, *A Decade of Sculpture.,* Associated University Presses Inc., 1974.

Kerlow, Isaac, & Rosenbush, Judson. *Computer Graphics for Designers and Artists.* 2nd Ed. Van Nostrand Reinhold, 1994.

Shipley, James & Weller, Allen. *Contemporary American Painting and Sculpture.* University of Illinois Press, 1974.

Lucie-Smith,E. *Late Modern, The Visual Arts Since 1945.* Praeger Publishers, 1969.

Andrews, Oliver. *Living Materials,* University of California Press, 1983.

Pickover, Clifford A. *Mazes for the Mind.* St. Martin's Press, 1992.

Lawrence, Sidney. *Music in Stone: Great Sculpture Gardens of the World.* Sidney, Scala Publications, 1985.

Thalacker, Donald, *The Place of Art in the World of Architecture,* Chelsea House Publishers.1980. Preface by Sam Hunter, Princeton University.

Newman, Thelma R. *Plastics as an Art Form.* Chilton Book Company, 1969.

Hollander, Harry. *Plastics for Artists & Craftsmen.* Watson-Guptill Publications, 1972.

Redstone, Louis G. *Public Art.* McGraw Hill Books, 1981.

Miller, Teressa. *The Security Pacific Collection.* Security Pacific Corp., 1985.

Kowal, Dennis & Meilach, Donna. *Sculpture Casting.* Crown Publishers, 1972.

Williams, Arthur. *Sculpture: Technique-Form-Content.* Davis Publications, 1989.

Zelanski, Paul & Fisher, Pat. *Shaping Space.* Harcourt Brace, 1994.

CATALOGUES (chronological order) / KATALOGE (chronologisch)

The Oakland Museum. *Northern California Sculptors Annual.* 1960.

San Francisco Museum of Modern Art. *Twenty-fourth Annual Drawing, Print and Sculpture Exhibition.* Foreword by George D. Culler. San Francisco, California. 1961.

The Museum of Modern Art. *Painting and Sculpture Acquisitions.* New York. 1963.

Musee d'Art Moderne de la Ville de Paris. *Biennale de Paris 1963; Onze Sculpteurs Americains.* Introduction by Herschel B. Chipp. 1963.

La Jolla Museum of Art.*Some Aspects of California Painting & Sculpture.* Introduction by Donald Brewer. La Jolla, California 1965.

Marin Museum Association. *The Growing Edge of California Sculpture.* San Rafael, California. 1965.

Lytton Center of the Visual Arts. *Contemporary Art from the Lytton Collection.* Los Angeles. 1966.

Richmond Art Center. *13000 Pounds of Outdoor Art.* Richmond, California. 1966.

Lytton Center of the Visual Arts. *California Artists in National Collections.* Los Angeles, California. 1967.

Hansen Gallery. *Plastics West - Coast.* San Francisco. 1967.

Richmond Art Center. *Thirtieth Anniversary Exhibition.* Richmond, California. 1967.

Franklin D. Murphy Sculpture Garden. *Catalog of the Collection.* University of California at Los Angeles. 1968.

Krannert Art Museum, University of Illinois. *Contemporary American Painting and Sculpture 1969.* Introduction by James R. Shipley and Allen S. Weller. Urbana, Illinois. 1969.

Milwaukee Art Center. *A Plastic Presence.* Introduction by Tracy Atkinson. Milwaukee, Wisconsin. 1969.

McNay Art Institute. *Plastics and New Art.* Introduction by Stephen S. Prokopoff. San Antonio, Texas.1969.

Sheldon Memorial Art Gallery, University of Nebraska. *American Sculpture.* Essay by Norman A. Geske. Lincoln, Nebraska. 1970.

The Oakland Museum. *Pierres de Fantaisie.* Foreword by George Neubert. Oakland, California. 1970.

Joslyn Art Museum. *Looking West 1970.* Introduction by LeRoy Butler. Omaha, Nebraska. 1970.

Crocker Art Museum. *1970 Biennial Invitation: West Coast '70 Painters and Sculptors.* Sacramento, California. 1970.

Stanford University Museum of Art and the Santa Barbara Museum of Art. *A Decade in the West: Painting, Sculpture and Graphics from the*

Anderson Collection. Introduction by Albert E. Elsen. Palo Alto, California. 1971.

M.H. de Young Memorial Museum and the California Palace of the Legion of Honor. *Bruce Beasley: An Exhibition of Acrylic Sculpture.* Introduction by William H. Elsner. San Francisco, California. 1972.

Le Salon de Mai. *Biennial Exhibition.* Introduction by Gaston Diehl. Paris, France. 1973.

Salon de la Jeune Sculpture XXV. *Biennial Exhibition.* Introduction by Denys Chevalier. Paris, France. 1973.

Saint Mary's College Art Gallery. "The Small Format". Moraga, California. 1973.

DeCordova Museum. *Refracted Images.* Wooster, Massachusetts. 1973.

Krannert Art Museum, University of Illinois. *Contemporary American Painting and Sculpture 1974.* Introduction by James R. Shipley & Allen S. Weller. Urbana, Illinois. 1974.

The Oakland Museum. *Public Sculpture/Urban Environment.* Introduction by George Neubert. Oakland, California. 1974.

Franklin D. Murphy Sculpture Garden. *Catalog of the Collection.* University of California at Los Angeles. 1976.

US General Service Administration. *Art in Architecture Program.* Washington, D.C. 1978, 1979.

Dartmouth College Museum & Galleries. *Acquisitions 1974-1978.* Introduction by Jan van der Marck. Hanover, New Hampshire. 1979.

Walnut Creek Civic Arts Gallery. *Spaces.* Introduction by Carl Worth. Walnut Creek, California. 1979.

National Museum of American Art, Smithsonian Institution. *Across the Nation: Fine Art for Federal Buildings,* 1972-79. Introduction by Joshua C. Taylor. Washington. D.C. 1980.

Spencer Museum of Art, University of Kansas. *Catalogue of the Sculpture Collections.* Introduction by Douglas Hyland. Lawrence, Kansas. 1981.

The Oakland Museum. *100 Years of California Sculpture.* Introductions by Christina Orr-Cahall, Paul Tomidy, Terry St. John. Oakland, California. 1982.

DeSaisset Museum, University of Santa Clara. *Northern California Art of the Sixties.* Essays by Fred Martin, Georgianna Lagoria. Santa Clara, California. 1982.

University of Hawaii. *The First International Shoebox Sculpture Exhibition.* Introduction by Tom Kolbe. 1982.

Art Museum Association. *Forgotten Dimension... A Survey of Small Sculpture in California Now.*

Introduction by George W. Neubert. Organized by Fresno Art-Center. Fresno, California. 1982.

The Johnson Foundation. *Wingspread: The Sculpture Collection.* Racine, Wisconsin. 1983.

San Francisco Museum of Modern Art, *Spring Auction,* San Francisco, California, 1983

International Arts Foundation. *California Sculpture Show.* Foreword by Henry Hopkins; Essays by Jan Butterfield and Melinda Wortz. Olympic Arts Festival, Los Angeles, California. 1984.

Franklin D. Murphy Sculpture Garden. *Catalog of the Collection.* University of California at Los Angeles. Essay by Gerald Nordland. 1984.

Euphrat Gallery, De Anza College. *Art Collectors in and Around Silicon Valley.* Essay by Jan Rindfleisch. Cupertino, California. 1985.

University of Oregon. *In Retrospect: The Oregon International Sculpture Symposium of 1974.* Eugene, Oregon. 1985.

Yorkshire Sculpture Park. *California Sculpture Show.* Introduction by Peter Murray. Yorkshire, England. 1985.

Kaiser Center. *Brook House Sculpture Invitational.* Introduction by George Neubert. Oakland, California. 1986.

Steel Sculpture Symposium. *Steel Sculpture.* Essay by Siegfried Salzmann. Park der Burg Linn, Germany. Middelheim Sculpture Park, Antwerp, Belgium. Yorkshire Sculpture Park, Great Britain. Kunsthalle Bremen, Germany. 1987-1988.

Anchorage Museum of History and Art. *Sculpture, Looking into Three Dimensions.* Forward by Patricia Wolf. Anchorage, Alaska. 1987.

Ministry of Culture of Hungary. *7th International Small Sculpture Exhibition of Budapest.* Essay by Janos Frank. Budapest, Hungary. 1987.

The Oakland Museum. *Oakland's Artists '90.* Introduction by Harvey Jones. Oakland, California. 1990.

Sonoma State University. *Bruce Beasley, An Exhibition of Bronze Sculpture.* Essay by Albert Elsen. Rhonert Park. California. 1990.

The Oakland Museum. *Oakland's Artists '90.* Introduction by Harvey Jones. Oakland, California. 1990.

City of Oakland, Public Art Program. *Beyond Fragments: After the Earthquake,* Introduction by Regina Almaguer. Oakland, California. 1990.

Galerie Utermann. *Vernissage.* Dortmund, Germany. 1991.

Muckenthaler Cultural Center. *Sculptural Perspectives for the Nineties.* Essay by John Natsoulas. Fullerton, California. 1991.

The Utsukushi-ga-hara Open-Air-Museum. *The Fujisankei Biennale.* Essay by Sam Hunter. Tokyo, Japan. 1993.

Galerie Scheffel. *Bruce Beasley: March 1993,* Essay by Dr. Manfred Fath, Bad Homburg, Germany.

Galerie Utermann. *Bruce Beasley:* Essay by Dr. Gottlieb Leinz, September, 1993, Dortmund, Germany

EDITED ARTICLES AND REVIEWS (chronological order) / ZEITSCHRIFTEN (chronologisch)

Artforum. "Contemporary Painting and Sculpture: Everett Ellin Gallery". David Gebhard. April, 1962.

Los Angeles Times. "Beasley Sculpture on View at N.Y. Museum of Modern Art". December 16, 1962.

Oakland Tribune. "N.Y. Museum Gets Oakland Work". Miriam D. Cross. December 16, 1962.

Artforum. "A Portfolio of California Sculptors". John Coplans. April, 1963.

Artforum. "The 1963 Paris Biennale". Herschel B. Chipp. April, 1963.

Artforum., "Casting in the Bay Area". Joseph Pugliese. April, 1963.

Arts. "Prospect Over the Bay", A. Ventura, May 1963.

Los Angeles Times. "Young Sculptor Displays Rare, Precocious Talent". Henry J. Seldis. June 3, 1963.

Los Angeles Herald Examiner. "Beasley's Textured Metal and Space". Arthur Miller. June 6, 1963.

Los Angeles Times. "International Group of Sculptors on View". Henry J. Seldis. June 28, 1963.

New York Herald Tribune. "Far-Out Sculpture Far Out West". Emily Genauer. August 11, 1963.

The New York Times. "California Sculptors Enter Paris Show". Lawrence E. Davies. September 11, 1963.

San Francisco Examiner. "A Paris Accolade". February 3, 1964.

Berkeley Dailey Gazette, "French Government Buys Sculpture by UC Artist". February, 3, 1964.

San Francisco Chronicle. "A French Honor". February 4, 1964.

Oakland Tribune. "U.C. Sculpture Returns from Paris Triumph". Miriam D. Cross. February 16, 1964.

California Monthly. "Sculpture in the Berkeley Mold". Paul Thayer. April, 1964.

New York Herald Tribune. "Review". October 3, 1964.

The New York Times. "Review". Stuart. Preston. October 3, 1964.

Artnews, "Bruce Beasley: Review ". Jill Johnson. November, 1964.

Art International. "Review" Barbara Rose, November, 1964.

San Francisco Examiner. "Top Prize to Oakland Sculptor". Lynn Ludlow. May 2, 1965.

Los Angeles Times. "Locals Get Chance in Lytton Exhibit", Henry Seldis, 1965.

Oakland Tribune. "First Big Show by Marin Art Group". Miriam D. Cross. May 16, 1965.

San Francisco Chronicle, "Beasley's Art Ennobles 'Junk". Dean Wallace. October 19, 1965.

Artforum, "San Francisco Review". E.M. Polly. December, 1965.

Los Angeles Times. "Beasley, Zammitt Shows Outstanding". Henry J. Seldis. January 10, 1966.

Artforum. "Bruce Beasley". William Wilson. March 1966.

San Francisco Sunday Examiner and Chronicle, "A Foundry in His Own Back Yard". Walter Blum. March 13, 1966.

San Francisco Chronicle, "Sculptors Who Operate Their Own Foundries". Alfred Frankenstein. March 16, 1966.

The Milwaukee Journal. "Artist Casts Own Creations". staff writer. February 19, 1967.

San Francisco Chronicle. "Arts Festival Names Winners". staff writer. September 22, 1967.

San Francisco Examiner. "Gimmicks and Beauty in Art Out of Plastics". Arthur Bloomfield. November 3, 1967.

Artforum., . "Plastics West Coast". Palmer D. French. January 1968.

Time Magazine. "The Crystal Clear Scene". Ralph Graves. February 9, 1968.

Oakland Tribune. "Bruce Beasley's Studio". Joan Palm. September 29, 1968.

Forth Worth Star Telegram. "Young Artist's Work Exhibited in Dallas". James Meeker. October 20, 1968.

Los Angeles Times. "Sculptor Unveils Impossible Feat". William Wilson. March 15, 1969.

Time Magazine. "Ars Gratic Amoris". Ralph Graves. July 11, 1969.

The New York Times. "Building the Plastic Image". Grace Glueck. December 7, 1969.

The Sacramento Bee. "Big clear Sculpture..." Charles Johnson. December 12, 1969.

Oakland Tribune, "A Satirical Brutal View of Pollution". Miriam Duncan Cross. January 25, 1970.

San Francisco Sunday Examiner and Chronicle. "A Statue

for the State". Thomas Albright. February 8, 1970.

Los Angeles Times, "Sculptor Unveils 'Impossible' Feat". William Wilson. March 15, 1970.

S2acramento Union. "Huge Sculpture Marks Advance for Art". Richard. Simon. March 14, 1970.

The Sacramento Bee. "Apolymon - A Triumph of Sculpture". March 14, 1970.

The San Diego Union. "Capital Unveils Plastic Sculpture". March 15, 1970.

The Sacramento Bee. "Apolymon - A Major Happening in City History". Charles Johnson. March 22, 1970.

Artweek. "Apolymon Flies on Light", DeWitt Robbeloth. March 15, 1970.

Oakland Tribune, "Oakland Sculptor Bruce Beasley in Capital", Miriam Duncan Cross. *March 22, 1970.*

Sacramento Union, "Huge Sculpture Marks Advance for Art, State", Richard Simon, March 27, 1970.

San Francisco Sunday Examiner and Chronicle." It's the Man, Not the Medium". Walter Blum. April 19, 1970.

Artforum. "San Francisco: Beasley Sculpture Between State Office Buildings". J.Tarshis, Summer 1970.

Artnews. "The Age of Lucite Dawns in Sacramento". Ed Hotaling. May 1970.

San Francisco Chronicle. "The Funkiest Show in Town". staff writer. May 3, 1970.

San Francisco Sunday Examiner and Chronicle. "American Sculpture in Perspective". Alfred Frankenstein. September 27, 1970.

San Francisco Chronicle."Plastics as Fine as Marble". Alfred Frankenstein. October 29, 1970.

Artweek. "Solidified Atmospheres". Cecile N. McCann. November 7, 1970.

Oakland Tribune. " Sparkling Show at the Oakland Museum". Miriam D. Cross. November 15, 1970.

San Francisco Chronicle. "An Impressive Look West". Thomas Albright. November 29, 1970.

San Francisco Sunday Examiner and Chronicle. "Fascinating Sculpture Full of Invention". Alfred Frankenstein. February 14, 1971.

Art Gallery Magazine."Review". Thomas Albright. Vol. XIV, no. 6, March 1971.

San Francisco Chronicle. "*Bay Area Medicis*". Thomas Albright. June 12, 1971.

San Francisco Chronicle. "One and a Half Tons of Lucite". July 15, 1972.

Oakland Tribune. "Museum Installs Beasley Sculpture". Miriam D. Cross. July 16, 1972.

San Francisco Examiner. "New Oakland Acquisition". July 17, 1972.

Daily Review. "Dioptus Sculpture Adds Naked Poetry..", Gary Tischkler. Hayward, California. July 26, 1972.

Daily Review. "Sculptor Makes His Work an Integral Part of Life", Gary Tischler, Hayward, Ca., August 2, 1972.

Artweek.. "Bruce Beasley, Sculptor of Light". Cecile N. McCann, August 26, 1972.

Palo Alto Times, "Master Sculptor Shows Acrylics", staff writer, September 29, 1972.

Vallejo Times-Herald, "Bruce Beasley's Acrylic Sculpture to be Exhibited at De Young Museum". E.M. Polly, October 1, 1972.

Artweek, "Bruce Beasley at De Young Museum". Cecile McCann. October 21, 1972.

San Francisco Examiner. "Acrylic Makes Good Art". Arthur Bloomfield. October 14, 1972.

San Francisco Chronicle. "Some New Artistic Directions". Alfred Frankenstein. October 21, 1972.

Oakland Tribune. "Beasley Exhibit Glitters and Glistens". Miriam D. Cross. November 26, 1972.

Art Gallery Magazine. "Review".Thomas Albright. Vol. XVI, no. 3, December 1972.

Santa Barbara News Press. "Lucite Sculpture by Beasley at Museum". January 7, 1973.

Los Angeles Times. "Beasley Sculpture on View". Henry J. Seldis, January 22, 1973.

T*he San Diego Union,* "Transparent Sculpture Here". Carol Olten. March 4, 1973.

Recherchre & Architecture: Annee 1973, "Bruce Beasley, Sculpteur". Paris, France, 1973.

Boston Sunday Globe. "DeCordova trips the light fantastic". Robert Taylor. February 18, 1973.

The Oregonian, "Sculptors, Public Involved in Art for Oregon". Beth Fagan. Portland, Oregon, July 18, 1974.

Register -Guard, "Symposium Sculptors and their Works". Mike O'Brien. Eugene, Oregon, July 21, 1974.

Artweek, "Sculptures for Public Places". Mike E. Walsh. September 7, 1974.

San Francisco Chronicle. .."The Undersea World of Bruce Beasley's Bathysphere". Beth Coffelt. Feb. 1, 1976.

San Francisco Examiner. "Sculptors Scientific Hit". staff writer. February 26, 1976.

Sculptor's News Exchange. "Beasley Turns from Acrylic to Aluminum". Herk Van Tongeren. May, 1978.

Oakland Tribune. "Oakland Sculptor Wins $139,000 Commission". Wanda McClarin. November 9, 1979.

San Bernardino Sun. "Newest Sculpture Brings Questions". Ray Cooklis. June 20, 1980.

Oakland Tribune. "Capital Exhibit for Oakland Artist". Charles Shere. June 21, 1980.

San Bernardino Sun. "Sculptor Expects Work to Outlast Criticism". Ray Cooklis. June 27, 1980.

San Francisco Business Journal. "Sculptor Bruce Beasley". Harre W. Demoro. March 23, 1981.

Artweek. "Bruce Beasley: New Work, New Medium". Andree Marechal-Workman. June 20, 1981.

San Francisco Chronicle, "The Multi-Faceted World of Sculptor Bruce Beasley". Allan Temko. June 20, 1981.

Nob Hill Gazette. "A Trio in the Galleries". Mary Stofflet. July, 1981.

The Grand Rapids Press. "Shoebox Sculptures". Bernice Mancewicz. July 25, 1982.

Peninsula Times Tribune. "Reviving Northern California Art of the Sixties". David Winter, Nov. 2, 1982.

Science '83. "The Sculpture Transparent". Michael. Rogers, December 1983.

Anchorage Daily News, "Public Art", Jan Ingram, Anchorage, Alaska, January 8, 1984.

Oakland Tribune. "California Sculpture Goes to the Olympics". Charles Shere. May 27, 1984.

Los Angeles Times. '' Sculpture on a Pedestal". Suzanne Muchnic. June 2, 1984.

Los Angeles Life-Daily News. "California Sculpture Show". Diana Rico. June 2, 1984.

Los Angeles Herald Examiner. ''California Sculpture for the World to See". Hunter Drohojowska. June 8, 1984.

Los Angeles Reader. "Art from California's Sixties Stars".Pamela Hammond. June 15, 1984.

The Milwaukee Journal. "Sculpturally Speaking, L.A.'s in Great Shape". Tom Strini. July 8, 1984.

Los Angeles Times. "A Potpourri of California Sculpture". William Wilson. June 17, 1984.

Horizon Magazine. "The Shape of Things". Susan Jones. June 1984.

The San Diego Union. "Show is Olympian in size". David Lewubsin. July 8, 1984.

Artweek, "The Olympics California Sculpture Show", John Blumfield, July 28, 1984.

Arts & Architecture. "California Sculpture Show". Barbara Goldstein. December 1984.

Mannheimer Lokalnachrichten. "Die Skulpturen Show aus Kalifornien". B.Steigler. February 1, 1985. Germany

Rhein-Neckar-Main. "California Sculpture Show". February 1, 1985.

Die Welt. "Zwölf Bildhauer in der California Sculpture Show". Herbert Albrecht. February 18, 1985. Germany

Frankfurter Allgemeine Zeitung. "California Sculpture Show". February 20, 1985. Germany

Mannheimer Morgen, "Wenn die Linie einen Bogen kreuzt". Alfred Huber. February 21, 1985. Germany

Rhein-Neckar-Zeitung. "Olympischer Nachgeschmack". Isabelle v. Neumann. March 5, 1985. Germany

Suddeütsche Zeitung. "Kunst von der Olympiade". Doris Schmidt, March 5, 1985, Germany

Wakefield Express. "Bretton display of sculptures from California". Janet Barnfather. May 10, 1985. England

Yorkshire Post. "California Sculpture Show". May 16, 1985. England

Huddersfield Daily Examiner. "California Creations...". May 17, 1985. England

Sheffield Morning Telegraph. "All Things Californian", May 21, 1985, England

Morning Telegraph "All Things Californian"Maggie Lett, May 21, 1985. Sheffield, England

The Star, "From California to West Bretton", Michael Field, May 27, 1985, Yorkshire, England

Contra Costa Times. "Beasley sculpture invites closer look". Carol Fowler. May 4, 1986.

The Montclarion. "Oakland artists exhibit monumental sculptures". September 2, 1986.

Reinische Post. "Dokumente der Zeit in Stahl". Hans Martin Frese. May 26, 1987. Germany

Westdeutche Zeitung. "Stahl Gibt der Natur elnen Starken Akzent". Frank Lingnau. June 29, 1987. Germany

Die Welt. "Am Liebsten mit Rost". Peter Ditmar. September 17, 1987. Germany

Rheinische Post. "Burgpark, Kunstpark, Spielpark". Petra Kull. October 3, 1987. Germany

Handelsblatt. "Dokumente der Zeit". Klaus U. Reinke. October 11, 1987. Germany

Grand Forks Herald. "Bruce Beasley: Renaissance Man". Greg Booth. March 31, 1988.

Oakland Museum Magazine. Cover Illustration. October 1989.

The New York Times . "In Oakland Spaces for Art & Life". Julie Lew. February 4, 1990.

Los Angeles Times. "Art", Shauna Snow. April 29, 1990.

Alameda Times-Star. "Out of the Rubble", Janet Kornblum. May 2, 1990.

Daily Ledger-Post Dispatch. "Bruce Beasley-Environmental Expressionism". Sheila Wright. August 5,1990.

The Press-Enterprise. "Bruce Beasley Explores New Levels of Form". Mary A. Cline. October 28, 1990.

Elan Magazine. "Sculptor Bruce Beasley". November, 1990.

Houston Chronicle. "Sculpture Exhibit". Patricia Johnson. November 25, 1990.

Valley Times. "Oakland Artist Bruce Beasley". December 14, 1990.

Tri Valley Herald. "Sculpture a "landmark'". Mark van de Kamp. December 14, 1990.

Press Democrat. "Eye warms to Beasley...", Tim Fish. April 12, 1991.

San Jose Mercury News. "Urban Aesthetics". Robin Worthington. June 16, 1991.

Sacramento Magazine, "Sculptor Bruce Beasley". Dianne Heimer. February 1992.

The Christian Science Monitor. "Breaking Free of Artistic Labels". Marlena Donohue. July 27, 1992.

Oakland Museum Magazine. "Bruce Beasley, Recent Sculpture". Abby Wasserman. Summer 1992.

Peninsula Times Tribune. "The hills are alive with art". Tom Scanlon. July 14, 1992.

Sculpture Magazine. "Bruce Beasley". Marlena Donahue. July-August 1992.

The Modesto Bee, "Beasley's Artistic Vision". Leo Stutzin. September 20, 1992.

Sun-Sentinel, "Beasley Knows the Scale". Roger Hurlburt. Fort Launderdale, Florida. September 27, 1992.

Nike. "Bruce Beasley's Sculpture: Symbiosis of Nature and Technology ". Susanne Holst-Steppat. January/February 1993. Germany

Taunus-Zeitung "Konstrukteur von Bewegung: Der Bildhauer Bruce Beasley". Susanne Holst-Steppat. March 11, 1993. Germany

Tanus-Kurier. "Kubische Anordnungen in körperhafter Durchdringung". March 13, 1993. Germany

Oakland Museum Magazine. "Open to Question". Kate Neri. Summer, 1993.

Ruhr Nachrichten. "Bildhauer Bruce Beasley in der Galerie Utermann". September 1, 1993. Germany

Westfälischer Anzeiger. "Kristallreihen aus dem Computer". Ralf Stiftel, September 1, 1993. Germany

Westdeutsche Allgemeine. "Galerie Utermann zeigt Skulpturen von Bruce Beasley". September 1, 1993. Germany

Westfälische Rundschau, "Bruce Beasley-Skulptur aus einem Guß". Von Rainer Wanzelius. September 1, 1993. Germany

The Santa Fe New Mexican. "Beasley's Creations...". John Villani. September 16, 1993

Artis. "Stabil Und Doch Im Aufbruch: Der Bilhauer Bruce Beasely". Helga Boss-Stenner, February/ March 1994. Germany

Katalog Bruce Beasley

Städtische Kunsthalle Mannheim
Moltkestraße 9
68165 Mannheim
Geöffnet: Täglich 10 - 17 Uhr; Donnerstag 12 - 17 Uhr;
Montag geschlossen

© Copyright 1994

Städtische Kunsthalle Mannheim
Künstler und Autoren

Redaktion: Bruce Beasley
Autoren: Manfred Fath, Peter Selz
Übersetzungen: Barbara Buderer

Fotos: page 2: Leo Holub
        page 162, 175: Joanne Leonard
        alle photos de metallskulpturen 1987 - 1994 außer
        Intersections, Keystone und Bateleur II: Lee Fatheree

        all photos of metal sculptures 1987-1994
        except Intersections, Keystone and Bateleur II: Lee Fatheree

Druck: Pearl River Printing Company, Ltd., Hong Kong

Umschlagabbildung: Refuge, bronzeguß (cast bronze), 1993   (another view see page 146)

ISBN: 3-89165-098-2